The English Project

Stage One

Other Worlds
Edited by Donald Ball

Things Working
Edited by Penny Blackie

Family and School
Edited by David Jackson

Ventures
Edited by Elwyn Rowlands

I Took my Mind a Walk
Edited by George Sanders

Creatures Moving
Edited by Geoffrey Summerfield

Stage Two

Danger!
Edited by Norman Beer (spring 1977)

Good Time
Edited by Margaret Hewitt

Openings
Edited by Alex McLeod

The Receiving End
Edited by Peter Medway

That Once was Me
Edited by Dennis Pepper

Alone
Edited by George Robertson

Stage Three

Identity
Edited by Myra Barrs

Making Contact . . . and Breaking It
Edited by Pat D'Arcy (spring 1977)

The English Project

Edited by Alex McLeod

Stage Two **Openings**

Ward Lock Educational

First published as the Penguin English Project
by Penguin Books 1972
This edition published by Ward Lock Educational 1976

ISBN 0 7062 3532 0

Designed by Ivan Atanasoff
Set in Monophoto Apollo
by Oliver Burridge Filmsetting Ltd, Crawley
and printed by Ebenezer Baylis and Son, Worcester
for Ward Lock Educational
116 Baker Street, London W1M 2BB
Made in Great Britain

Contents

Before one goes through the gate

Before one goes through the gate
one may not be aware there is a gate
One may think there is a gate to go through
and look a long time for it
without finding it
One may find it and
it may not open
If it opens one may be through it
As one goes through it
one sees that the gate one went through
was the self that went through it
no one went through a gate
there was no gate to go through
no one ever found a gate
no one ever realized there was never a gate.

R. D. Laing

My thoughts

I sometimes wonder what my mind is like inside, often I fancy that it is like this. I feel as if my mind goes round and round like the earth and if my lessons make me think hard it begins to spin. In my other class it was getting all stodgy and still and lumpy and rusty. I feel as if there is a ball in my mind and it is divided into pieces – each piece stands for a different mood. The ball turns every now and then and that's what makes me change moods. I have my learning mood, my goodlooks mood, my happy mood, my loose-end mood and my grumpy mood, my missrable mood, my thoughtful mood and my planning mood. At the moment I am writing this I am in my thoughtful mood. When I am in my thoughtful mood I think out my maths and plan stories and poems. When my kitten is in her thoughtful mood she thinks shall I pounce or not, and shall I go to sleep or not. This sort of thing goes on in my own mind too. It is very hard for me to put my thoughts into words.

Sarah Gristwood *aged 7*

You're

Clownlike, happiest on your hands,
Feet to the stars, and moon-skulled,
Gilled like a fish. A common-sense
Thumbs-down on the dodo's mode.
Wrapped up in yourself like a spool,
Trawling your dark as owls do.
Mute as a turnip from the Fourth
Of July to All Fools' Day,
O high-riser, my little loaf.

Vague as fog and looked for like mail.
Farther off than Australia.
Bent-backed Atlas, our travelled prawn.
Snug as a bud and at home
Like a sprat in a pickle jug.
A creel of eels, all ripples.
Jumpy as a Mexican bean.
Right, like a well-done sum.
A clean slate, with your own face on.

Sylvia Plath

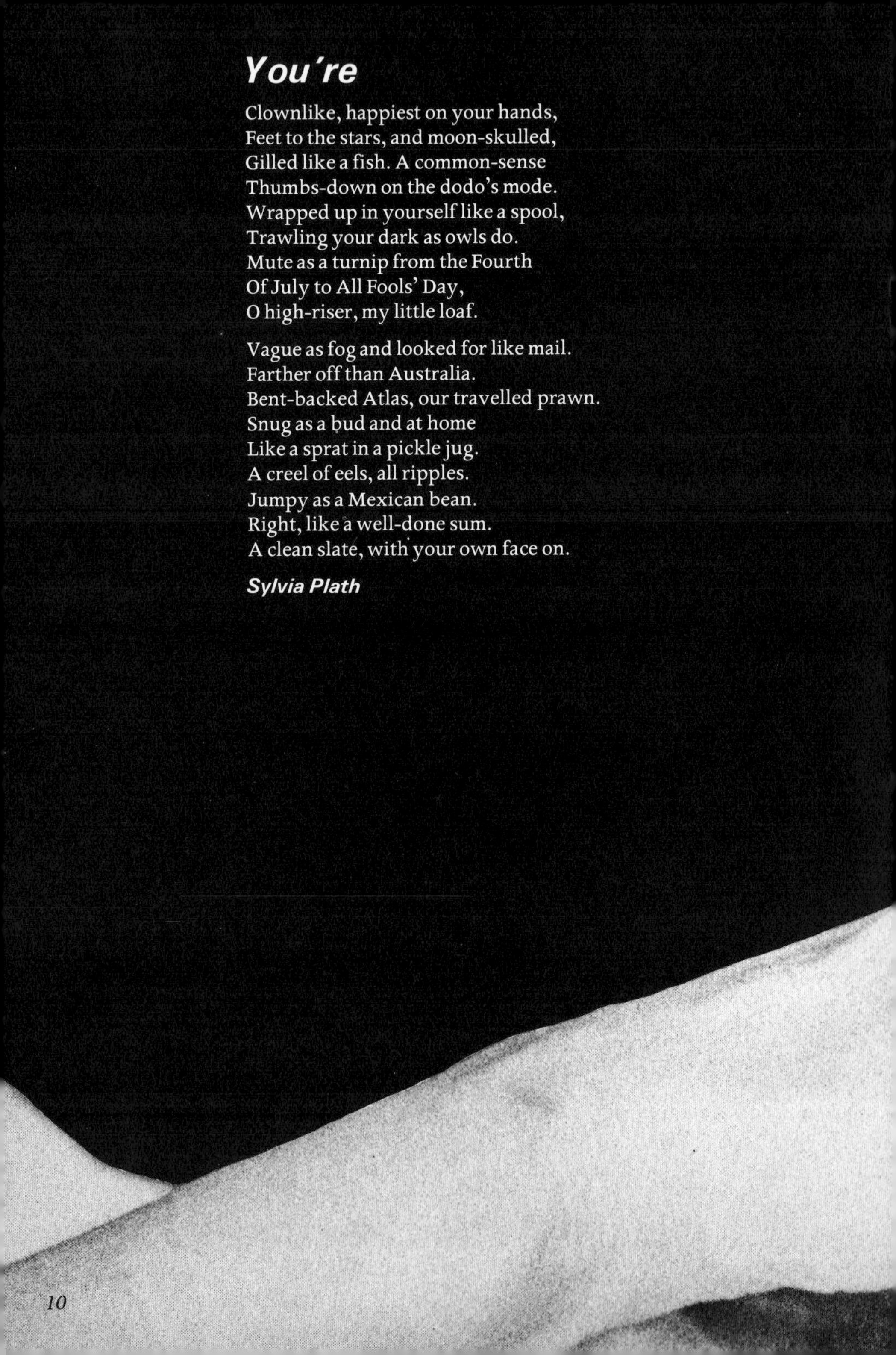

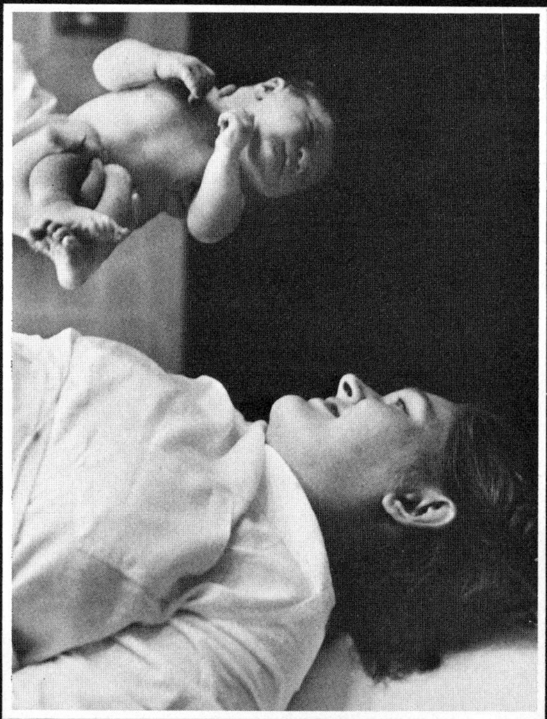

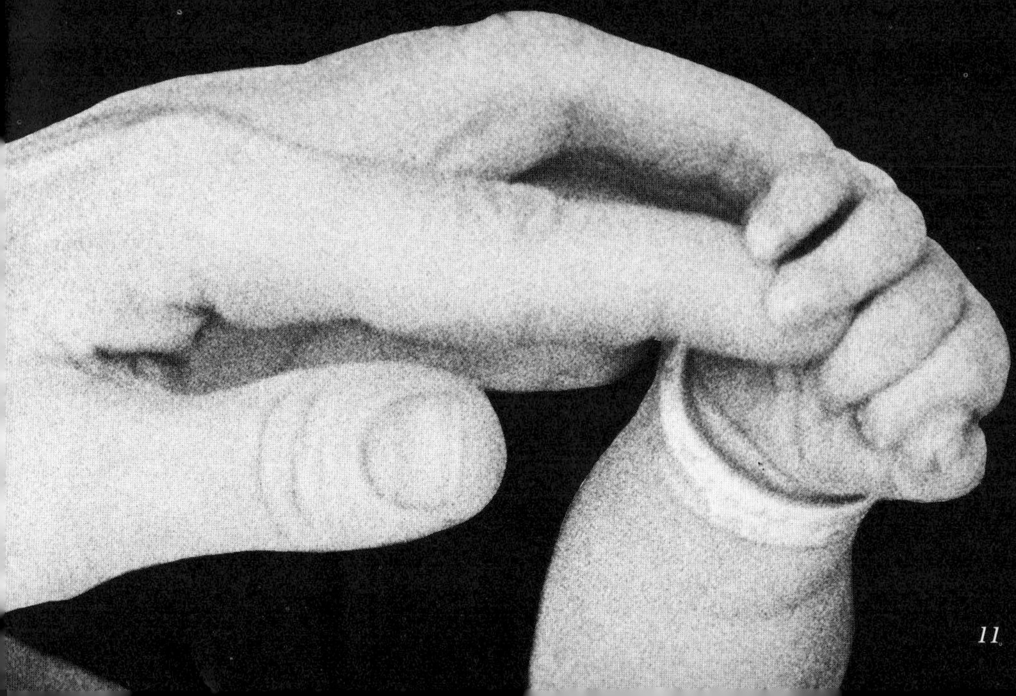

He and I

He's always warm; I'm always cold. In summer, when it is really hot, he never stops complaining how hot he is. If he sees me putting on a jersey in the evening, he's scornful.

He speaks several languages well; I don't speak a single one properly. Even languages he doesn't know he manages to speak in a way of his own.

He has a good sense of direction; I have none. After a day in a town abroad he gets about as carefree as a butterfly. I get lost in my own town, and have to ask how to get myself home. He hates asking the way; when we drive about towns we don't know he refuses to ask the way and tells me to look at the map. I can't read maps, I get all tangled up in those little red circles and he gets angry.

He isn't shy; I am. Sometimes I've seen him shy, though. With policemen, when they come up to our car armed with notebook and pencil. With them he turns shy, feeling he's in the wrong.

And even not feeling in the wrong. I think he feels respectful towards established authority.

I'm scared of established authority, and he isn't. He respects it. That's different. If I see a policeman coming along to fine us, I think straight away he's going to drag us off to prison. Prison doesn't enter his head; but out of respect he grows timid and agreeable.

To me, every activity is extremely hard, wearisome, uncertain. I'm very lazy, and if I want to get through anything I've simply got to spend long hours lazing on a sofa. He never lazes, he's always doing something; he types at top speed with the wireless on; when he goes to lie down in the afternoon, he takes along proofs to correct or a book of notes; on the one day he wants us to go to the cinema, then to a party, then to the theatre. In a single day he manages to do, and to make me do as well, any number of different things; to meet the most disparate people; and if I'm alone and try to do as he does, I can't manage anything, because I stay stuck for the whole afternoon where I meant to stop for half an hour, get lost and can't find the way, or because the dreariest person I least want to see drags me off to the place I least want to go to.

If I tell him what I've done with my afternoon he thinks it completely wasted, he's amused, teases me and gets annoyed; and says I'm hopeless without him.

I can't arrange my time. He can.

He has sudden rages that overflow like froth on a glass of beer. My tempers are sudden as well. But his pass off quickly; whereas mine leave a complaining, insistent trail behind them, which I think is tremendously irritating, a sort of bitter whine.

Sometimes, in the whirlwind of his temper, I weep; and far from softening and soothing him, my tears make him angrier than ever. He says they're all play-acting; and maybe he's right. Because, in the midst of my tears and his rages, I am completely calm.

Over my real sorrows I never weep.

At one time I would hurl plates and crockery on the floor in a rage. No longer now, though. Perhaps because I've grown older, and my rages are less violent; and then I wouldn't dare touch our plates now, as I'm fond of them and we bought them in London, one day, in the Portobello Road.

Natalia Ginzburg *Translated from the Italian by Isabel Quigly*

A Modest Proposal

There is no better way to know us
Than as two wolves, come separately to a wood.
Now neither's able to sleep – even at a distance
Distracted by the soft competing pulse
Of the other; nor able to hunt – at every step
Looking backwards and sideways, warying to listen
For the other's slavering rush. Neither can make die
The painful burning of the coal in its heart
Till the other's body and the whole wood is its own
Then it might sob contentment toward the moon.

Each in a thicket, rage hoarse in its labouring
Chest after a skirmish, licks the rents in its hide,
Eyes brighter than is natural under the leaves
(Where the wren, peeping round a leaf, shrieks out
To see a chink so terrifyingly open
Onto the red smelting of hatred) as each
Pictures a mad final satisfaction.

Suddenly they duck and peer.
                                        And there rides by
The great lord from hunting. His embroidered
Cloak floats, the tail of his horse pours,
And at his stirrup the two great-eyed greyhounds
That day after day bring down the towering stag
Leap like one, making delighted sounds.

Ted Hughes

An Evening at the Garibaldi

Every Saturday night for half a century the women of Green Street gathered in the Snug of 'The Garibaldi'. It was a time of intimacy and relaxation, a time for mutual commiseration and sympathy, a time for gossip and scandal. But it was something else too. It became a time for self-justification against the outside world: among the peeling brown paint and the frosted glass and the stained wooden tables, their conversation evolved into a declaration of faith in themselves and the standards they lived by, an exposition of their profoundest beliefs and thoughts.

They greet each other with inquiries about their health and their family. The woman who had an operation ten years ago returns to it unfailingly. 'I'm bin ever so middling agen this week, but then what can y'expect after a packet like that?' but nobody pays any attention to her as she continues, 'Had to come away you see it did, the whole bag o'tricks. Tain't the sort o' thing you can expect to get over in five minutes.' They know she mustn't be indulged or she'll talk about it all night, so the conversation is adroitly turned to someone else.

'How's your mother keeping, Mrs Carter?'

'Well, you know, it's her age more'n anythink else.'

'Ow old is she now?'

'Eighty-three in the noo year. She's a bit of a trial, though.'

'Well, you're bound to be at that age.'

'Poor ole soul.'

'Yis, one foot in the grave, gal, one foot in the grave. . . .' Ad to laugh though yis'day – our Sandra said: yis she might be got one foot in the grave, but she's got the other bugger pretty firm in Green Street.'

'Don't 'spect she can get about much.'

'Sometimes she guz as fur as the Old Folks' Rest Centre. I'm thankful to see the back of 'er sometimes. She says she's got a long enough rest comin' as it is. Says she wun't see another winter after this 'un. Still, she's bin sayin' that for the last ten year.'

Mrs Carter says piously that she thinks sometimes that it'd be a mercy if the old lady was Took, and she admits that her husband says it'll be a happy release for him when she is. 'I mean, we shouldn't gain by it, it'd mean losin' 'er pension.'

They drink up mournfully, and hope they won't linger to be a burden to anybody.

A melancholy reflective silence is established that can only be broken by a complete change of subject. Somebody mentions last week's television play, and they suddenly become animated.

'It was that bad we had to turn it off.'

'What was it?'

'Merchant o' Bloody Venice. Bloody Shakespeare.'

'O, 'im,' says another knowingly, as if she were talking about the carryings-on of some disreputable acquaintance.

'Somebody ought to write up,' interjects one woman vehemently – a frequent suggestion when they imagined themselves in any way wronged or slighted. It never went beyond the stage of suggestion, chiefly because they had not the faintest idea of whom to apply to for redress of their grievance.

'Sid says it's scandalous. All them men dressed up in tights and dinxin' about like a lot o' nancy-boys and spoutin' a lot o' poetry.' There is a muttered echo of agreement, 'bloody poetry'. She gains confidence in her theme and pursues it indignantly. 'He reckons this age'll goo down in 'Ist'ry as the Omerseckshul Age. An' 'e ain't far wrong, if you ask me.'

'Did you see it, Mrs Watts? Just up your street, I bet, all them men in tights.'

'Goo on, she's too old for that, ain't yer, gal?'

'Don't you be so sure.'

'Still waters run deep, eh, Ida?'

They talk of poetry and art as if it were a conspiracy against them. Somebody remembers having read of a painting by 'that ole b. Picasso' which was sold for many thousands of pounds. 'I said to our Jack, "How would you like that b. starin' at you all day?", he said, "There's only one room in the house it's fit for," I said, "Well if that didn't make you goo nothing ever would."'

Mrs Plackett says that her husband wouldn't let her switch off *The Merchant of Venice*, and they turn towards her in sympathy. 'He says it's ever so good when you get to know the ins and outs of it.' They stare at her, startled and incredulous, waiting for the elucidation of this novel and unexpected response. But she is unable to account for it, and finishes apologetically, 'But then 'e's always bin a bit funny that way.'

'They don't know what it is to enjoy theirselves, people like that, do they?'

'I tell yer straight, gal' – and the drink releases long-repressed bitterness and tears of self-pity – 'and I don't care 'oo 'ears me say it' (an expression they always used prefatory to defiance of any accepted ideas) 'I wouldn't wish my worst enemy 'usband like I'm 'ad. I don't know 'ow I'm managed to stick it all these years. Our Geraldine says she'd 'ave divorced 'im long ago. Mental cruelty she says they call it. She makes no bones about it. 'E ain't bin no 'usband to me. . . .'

There is consternation among those assembled, less from a feeling of sympathy with what she must have suffered at the hands of a husband with highbrow pretensions, than from an awareness that she has introduced a topic that is not included in the area of public discussion. Someone tells her sharply, to pull herself together, and she subsides on a bench against the wall, embarrassed by the sudden realization that she has exceeded the bounds of propriety. The conversation becomes broken and disjointed. They had no response to unforeseen personal disclosures. Ritual public mourning and rejoicing marked the limit of their involvement with others. A stony incomprehension greeted everything else. If you suffered, you were expected to show resignation and fortitude, and to present to outsiders the uniform imperturbability of the rest of the street, who were released from any obligation to sympathise with you by the prudent and comforting belief that all suffering was self-inflicted anyway, and therefore a result of your own folly or wickedness. You had only yourself to blame. If a husband were cruel you shouldn't have married him, if your children were unloving you had failed to bring them up properly, if you were ill you were guilty of neglect, and a determined stoicism was the only admissible attitude.

'Other people's troubles', like other people's kids and other people's houses, were their own concern. A woman – a stranger – once collapsed on the pavement in the middle of Green Street. The indignant householder, whose doorstep had been selected for this act of negligence, trembled and fluttered behind her lace curtain for some minutes before offering the afflicted stranger asylum within her house. Afterwards, when the ambulance had transported the sick woman to hospital, and she saw her property undefiled by the fleeting presence of a stranger who had had a heart attack, she confided to the neighbours that she had been terrified. 'I was frit to death she was gunner die on me', as though it had been a premeditated action, and she carefully singled out as its victim.

People had to be discouraged from attempts to share their problems with you, or you might be forced to learn of whole unsuspected spheres of human suffering that would undermine everything you knew about human behaviour and experience.

They restore the disorbited conversation to its intended trajectory, with the panic and desperation with which they chase the escaped pet budgerigar as it flutters uncontrollably around the room and threatens to disappear through an open window. They turn to some sex crimes reported in the newspapers and at once harmony and unanimity are restored among them.

They are interrupted by someone collecting for a wreath for May Rayson. 'Sat 'ere she did, week in, week out, for the best part o' forty year.' Nobody could sing 'The Rose of Tralee' quite like she could, and nobody will again, at least not in 'The Garibaldi'. A melancholy silence is established, heightened by the sound of laughter from the bar and the clash of glasses. In an adjoining room the skittles fall and are set up again.

'Makes you wonder 'oo's gunner be next, dunnit?' The clamour is stilled for a moment as they look at each other. The falling flesh and thinning hair, swollen ankles and knotted hands. A woman pushes some strings of henna'd hair across her forehead, and another slouches forward on the hard stool. In the corner Granny Bray is crying silently into the dregs of her beer, and no-one pays any attention to her because they think she is drunk. But she is crying because she remembers a Sunday afternoon in July that seemed to last for ever, cool beer in an enamel jug, the rickety wooden chair on the hot pavement, a ham tea and the voices of children. She cries not because she regrets it, but for no other reason than that she remembers; it may be the smell of the beer that releases it, and it rises up in her like a strong choking vapour, forcing the present into oblivion.

dyed red

'Ardly seems possible, does it? I was talking to 'er only last Monday.'

'You're 'ere today and gone tomorrer.'

'And we ain't none of us gettin' no younger.... Look at me.... Lovely 'ead of 'air I used to 'ave – and she fingers her thin and tinted hair gently, as though afraid of damaging it further by her touch – 'I could sit on it when I was twenty. But not now, gal, not now.'

'What about me? I used to be real bonny.... But you wouldn't think so today....' And she raises a thin bare arm. 'Where's it all gone?' They talk with fear and wonder, as though they had been disfigured by some stealthy and undeclared enemy, like virgins ravished as they slept.

'Oo, for God's sake snap out of it. Don't start gettin' morbid of a Sat'day night' – as though there were an appointed weekly cycle of grief and joy. And she goes to the piano, urging them to sing. They do as she bids them, and then engender a spurious and artificial warmth. As they rock gently to and fro to the sound of the 'Merry Widow' Waltz, there is something hysterical in their gaiety, in the contrived protraction of a way of living which they know to be superseded and in decline....

Jeremy Seabrook *The Unprivileged*

MANN'S
PALE

Two Friends

I have something to tell you.
I'm listening.
I'm dying.
I'm sorry to hear.
I'm growing old.
It's terrible.
It is, I thought you should know.
Of course and I'm sorry. Keep in touch.
I will and you too.
And let know what's new.
Certainly, though it can't be much.
And stay well.
And you too.
And go slow.
And you too.

David Ignatow

Ogun

My uncle made chairs, tables, balanced doors on, dug out
coffins, smoothing the white wood out

with plane and quick sandpaper until
it shone like his short-sighted glasses.

The knuckles of his hands were sil-
vered knobs of nails hit, hurt and flat-

tened out with blast of heavy hammer. He was knock-knee'd, flat-
footed and his clip clop sandals slapped across the concrete

flooring of his little shop where canefield mulemen and a fleet
of Bedford lorry drivers dropped in to scratch themselves and talk.

There was no shock of wood, no beam
of light mahogany his saw teeth couldn't handle.

When shaping squares for locks, a key hole
care tapped rat tat tat upon the handle

of his humpbacked chisel. Cold
world of wood caught fire as he whittled : rectangle

window frames, the intersecting x of fold-
ing chairs, triangle

trellises, the donkey
box-cart in its squeaking square.

But he was poor and most days he was hungry.
Imported cabinets with mirrors, formica table

tops, spine-curving chairs made up of tubes, with hollow
steel-like bones that sat on rubber ploughs,

thin beds, stretched not on boards, but blue high-tensioned cables,
were what the world preferred.

And yet he had a block of wood that would have baffled them.
With knife and gimlet care he worked away at this on Sundays,

explored its knotted hurts, cutting his way
along its yellow whorls until his hands could feel

how it had swelled and shivered, breathing air,
its weathered green burning to rings of time,

its contoured grain still tuned to roots and water.
And as he cut, he heard the creak of forests :

green lizard faces gulped, grey memories with moth
eyes watched him from their shadows, soft

liquid tendrils leaked among the flowers
and a black rigid thunder he had never heard within his hammer

came stomping up the trunks. And as he worked within his
  shattered
Sunday shop, the wood took shape: dry shuttered

eyes, slack anciently everted lips, flat
ruined face, eaten by pox, ravaged by rat

and woodworm, dry cistern mouth, cracked
gullet crying for the desert, the heavy black

enduring jaw; lost pain, lost iron;
emerging woodwork image of his anger.

Edward Brathwaite

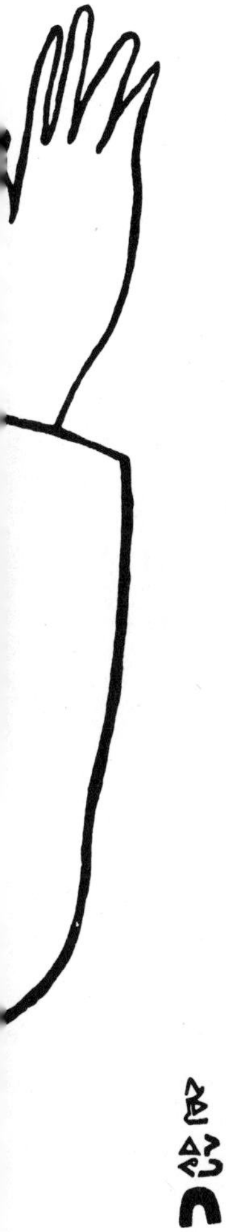

Uvlunaq's Song

A year or two before her son had murdered a hunting companion in a fit of temper, and he now lived an outlaw in the mountains. . . . And so his mother had made this song through sorrow over her son's fate.
Knud Rasmussen

Eya – eya.
I recognize
A bit of song
And take it to me like a fellow being.
Eyaya – eya.

Should I be ashamed
At the child I once carried
With me in my back-pouch,
Because I heard of his flight
From the haunts of man?
Eyaya – eya.

Truly I was ashamed:
But only because he had not
A mother who was as blameless as the blue sky,
Wise and without foolishness.
Now people's talk will educate him
And gossip complete the education.
I should perhaps be ashamed,
I, who bore a child
Who was not to be my refuge;
Instead, I envy those
Who have a crowd of friends behind them,
Waving on the ice,
When after festive leave-taking they journey out.
Oh, I remember a winter,
We left the island 'The squinting eye':
The weather was mild,
And the feet sank, gently creaking, into the thawing snow.
I was then as a tame animal among men;
But when the message came
Of the killing and the flight,
Then I staggered,
Like one unable to get a foothold.

Uvlunaq *Translated from the Eskimo by Knud Rasmussen and W. E. Calvert*

The Adams Family

At the end of the block, opposite The Common, and next to the abandoned Chinese joss-house, lives the Adams family whose design of private existence is so public and so different from my family's that I find it startling, outrageous and sometimes disgusting but, all in all, fascinating. There are never as many Adams children as there appear to be, and I recall only eight by name when I could, without torture, confidently have sworn to twice as many. Perhaps this multiplication is caused by their noise, their weasel-like dartings from place to place, and mostly by the fact that many of them seem about the same age, and strongly resemble each other. They are all knobbly at the joints and bony in between them, they are all knock-kneed, with gipsyish cheekbones, flat noses, long flexible mouths set in tide-lines of grime, unwinking beer-coloured eyes completely encircled by pink whites, and netted in wrinkles as though they are middle-aged. Boys and girls alike have spiky dust-brown hair in which burrs, chaff and streaks of jam or tomato sauce stick, and remain sticking, for days.

One or other is always shaven-headed because of lice. Granules like dried honey infest the corners of their eyes and the roots of their lashes. As all we country children do in summer, they go bare-footed, revealing long tarsier-like toes. In the colder months, when we others wear boots, they wear sandshoes that smell of feet. Their names strike me as glamorous and romantic, particularly the double names of the girls which are always used in full: Christobel Veronica, Rosalie Marigold, Geraldine Emily and Melba Florabelle. The boys' names are Winton, Aubrey, Selwyn and Maximilian.

squirrel

I am fully though astoundingly aware, from overhearing Mother and Father, that Mr Adams earns more money than Father, and therefore understand their possession of many things my parents very clearly express themselves as being too poor to afford. I observe, cold-eyed, that the Adams tribe places no value on domestic customs and rites of behaviour, I regard it as almost criminal to scant. In short: there is no fish-and-chip in the Bairnsdale of the nineteen-twenties, otherwise the Adamses would undoubtedly be fish-and-chip people. They have fish-and-chip manners.

On two occasions I somehow witness them at table. They do not wash before eating. There is no tablecloth, not even a newspaper one, and no table napkins. On each occasion there is the same centre piece, indubitably permanent, of bottles of tomato sauce, jars of sulphur-yellow pickles, tins of treacle and condensed milk, tins of jam with the lids jagged open and prised up by a tin-opener. All these vessels bleed and dribble on the greasy table. I know, from the conversations of the Adams children, that frankfurters, saveloys, sardines, bananas, garishly iced pastry-cook cakes, fresh bread and crumpets, are their favourite and most usual foods.

I see them feasting on black puddings, kola tonic and vanilla slices, champing loudly and quickly with their decayed teeth, giving no attention at all to any one of the many technicalities of eating Mother considers paramount. Knives are licked, mouths and noses wiped on sleeves, crusts are not eaten but thrown to the floor for the several dogs.

Mrs Adams, whom the older children call Ma and the younger Mumma, is put out by none of this. She is a taller but no plumper prophecy of what Christobel Veronica and the other girls will grow to, flatter of nose, spikier of hair, with the same unwinking eyes. As aitchless as her children she behaves as they do, dropping crusts lovingly to the dogs, slurping nigger-brown tea from a saucer, straining across the table to stab a knife into a tin of jam, and coating a slice of bread held flat on the palm of her hand with glutinious dollops of purple goo thus dug out. Her behaviour, more valid and impressing than her children's because she is a Mrs and a mother, shows me that there is an acceptable though different sort of family order, a different set of rules, a different conception of what is abundance.

The Adams idea of abundance is expressed in the five bicycles they own, in the several tricycles rusting with the rusting pilchard tins and Hornby railway lines and disintegrating go-carts among the shoulder-high weeds of the backyard, in the pianola and the stacks of unravelling pianola rolls, in the harmonium with *its* decayed teeth, the three banjos, the gramophone with its toffee-coloured convolvulus-shaped horn which seems repeatedly to wheeze out only Harry Lauder singing 'Roamin' in the gloamin' ' though there are deposits of records tossed like quoits in corners, on to pantry shelves, on to and under sofas.

I am not so much appalled as roused to wonder by seeing nothing in what I think is its right place: bicycle in the passage, fancy dress costumes and crutchless bloomers hanging on the backs of kitchen chairs, a sodden pillow and a doll's perambulator in the gully-trap, an iron saucepan containing the ashes of some long-age-charred Irish stew holding open the front door, playing cards in the lavatory, penny dreadfuls, kitten-decorated chocolate boxes and stone ginger-beer bottles everywhere.

The bedrooms really disconcert me. When I leave mine in the morning I do not enter it again until I am going to bed. It is a place I should not want to be in during the day. By training I regard a bedroom, then as now, as a spotless, uncluttered place to sleep in. The bedrooms of the Adams boys are junk-shop places to fight in, play in, store things in. Their unmade beds are littered with stamp albums, caramel papers, cigarette-cards and popguns. I am as astounded by a canary in a cage in one bedroom as I am by the presence of rabbit-traps, Meccano derricks, bicycle chains, boxing-gloves, an enamel plate half filled with a failure of toffee and an unemptied chamber-pot in which float apple-cores.

I am more startled, though I affect a form of polite deafness and blindness to it, by the almost formal litany of insult, tongue-poking-out (sharp, white tongues) and ugly-face-making that goes on between Mrs Adams and her children. I am used to the much less waspish form of bickering exchange, hearty and over-masculine, of my country uncles, and know that affection inspires it, and their matching adulthoods ratify it. It is clear too that Mrs Adams and her children, bitterly screeching at each other 'Greediguts' and 'Shut up, bum-face!' and 'Stinkpot!' and 'Youse is all barmy as bandicoots!' love each other, and regard their performances as conventional enough. Nevertheless, I am uneasy at this treatment of and by a parent, and am more uneasy because it is not something I am accidentally overhearing and seeing but something they do not consider caring if I see.

I am startled, too, that the Adams children and their dogs and dirt, and any neighbour, children and their dogs and dirt, have the run of the whole house, including the parental bedroom, and the use, at any odd time, without asking permission, of anything in the house – slices of bread-and-dripping, tins of condensed milk, the pianola, anything at all.

I am most startled by their friendly habit of offering to let me have a bite or suck from something they have already bitten or sucked – a pear, a piece of peppermint rock, a cheese sandwich, an aniseed ball. My nausea at the thought of accepting the offer is difficult to obscure even by a polite evasion of lies. Neither my stomach nor I has the moral strength to repay their insulting gesture of *bonhomie* with an insulting gesture of sacrifice. The nausea is caused partly by an inborn fastidiousness, partly by family training, but there is a cause so revolting that, whenever I am the subject of one of these offers to share, I need to escape quickly from the Adams circle until I carelessly forget the cause. The Adams boys blow their noses not with handkerchiefs but with their fingers. They use the same fingers, not paper, to wipe themselves.

Hal Porter *The Watcher on the Cast-Iron Balcony*

DOWN STAIRS FOR CITY (BANK)
AND LONDON TRANSPORT TRAINS
14
13
New Zealand
Cheddar
OVALTINE
ST. LUCIA

The Emigrants

So you have seen them
with their cardboard grips,
felt hats, rain-
cloaks, the women
with their plain
or purple-tinted
coats hiding their fatten-
ed hips.

These are The Emigrants.
On sea-port quays
at air-ports
anywhere where there is a ship
or train, swift
motor car, or jet
to travel faster than the breeze
you see them gathered :
passports stamped
their travel papers wrapped
in old disused news-
paper : lining their patient queues.

Where to ?
They do not know.
Canada, the Panama
Canal, the Miss-
issippi painfields, Florida ?
Or on to dock
at hissing smoke locked
Glasgow ?

Why do they go ?
They do not know.
Seeking a job
they settle for the very best
the agent has to offer :
jabbing a neighbour
out of work for four bob
less a week.

What do they hope for
what find there
these New World mariners
Columbus coursing kaffirs

What Cathay shores
for them are gleaming golden
what magic keys they carry to unlock
what gold endragoned doors ?

But now the doors are iron : mouldy
dredges do not care what we discover here :
the Mississippi mud is sticky :

men die there
and bouquets of stench lie
all night long along the river bank.

In London, Undergrounds are cold.
The train rolls in from darkness
with our fears

and leaves a lonely soft metallic clanking
in our ears.
In New York

nights are hot
in Harlem, Brooklyn,
along Long Island Sound

This city is so vast
its ears have ceased to know
a simple human sound

Police cars wail
like babies
an ambulance erupts

like breaking glass
an elevator sighs
like Jews in Europe's gases

then slides us swiftly
down the ropes to hell.
Where is the bell

that used to warn us,
playing cricket on the beach,
that it was mid-day : sun too hot

for heads ? And evening's
angelus of fish soup,
prayers, bed ?

The chaps who drive the City buses
don't like us clipping for them much ;
in fact, make quite a fuss.
Bus strikes loom soon.

The men who lever ale
in stuffy Woodbine pubs
don't like us much.
No drinks there soon.

Or broken bottles.
The women who come down
to open doors a crack
will sometimes crack

your fingers if you don't
watch out. Sorry!
Full! Not even Bread
and Breakfast soon

for curly-headed workers.
So what to do, man?
Ban the Bomb? Bomb
the place down?

Boycott the girls?
Put a ban on all
marriages? Call
You'self X

wear a beard
and a turban
washing your tur-
bulent sex
about six
times a day:
going Muslim?
Black as God

brown is good
white as sin?
An' doan forget Jimmy Baldwin
an' Martin Luther King. . . .

Our colour beats a restless drum
but only the bitter come.

Edward Brathwaite

SOLD
BY
STROUD

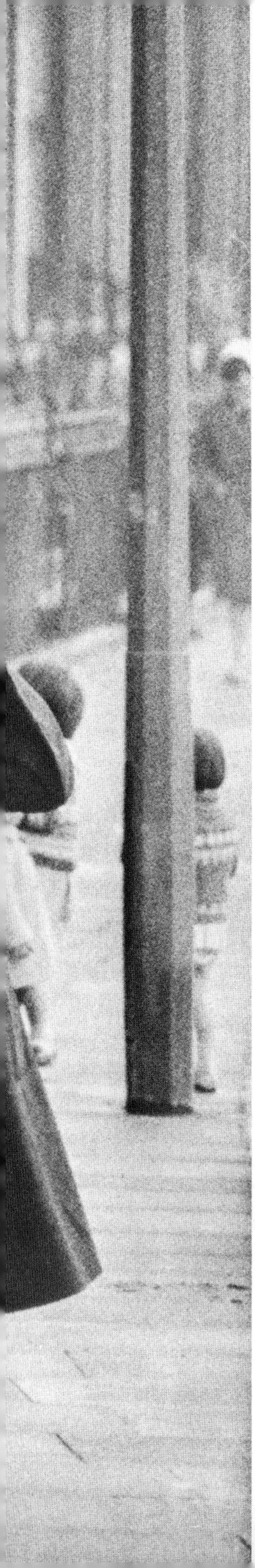

The Housing Lark

Now, I will have to digress with a ballad about Sylvester, which will help to explain why Syl ain't laughing. In the first place you mightn't think that Syl is an Indian, because he ain't have a Indian name, and a lot of people don't know it have true-true Indians living in the West Indies. Not *Carib* Indians or Red Indians, but Indians from India, wearing sari and thing. But some of them get so westernize that they don't even know where the Ganges is, and they pick up all sort of fancy name instead of the usual Singh or Ram.

One time Syl was catching real hell to get a room. He walking all over town reading the notice boards on the sweet shops and tobacconists, but all he could see is 'No Kolors' or 'Sorry, Uropean only.' Syl was thinking how is hell of a thing these people don't want him, when they can't even spell.

Well while he stand up there, the old Bat stroll along.

'What happening?' Bat say.

'I was looking for a place to live, man,' Syl say.

'You won't find nothing on them boards,' Bat say. 'But seeing that both of we is Trinidadians together, I will tell you of a place. Right up there by the next block, it have a house with an English landlord who taking Indians. He don't want any West Indians, mark you, but he taking real Indians. You could go there and try.'

'But I am from the West Indies,' Syl say.

'Nevertheless,' Bat say, 'you are an Indian. Why you don't go and try?'

'I don't too like living with a set of Indian people,' Syl grumble. 'So much of curry and dhal and kia-san-hai.'

'Well, is up to you.' Bat say.

In the end, after looking at some more notices, Syl decide to go to this house Bat tell him about. He knock at the door and stand up waiting for the landlord.

The landlord come and look at Syl suspiciously.

'Yes?' he say, as if Syl ask him a question and he answering 'yes'.
'I am straight from the banks of the Ganges,' Syl say. 'I am a student from the Orient seeking a roof over my head.'

'You are not wearing your national garments,' the landlord say.

'When you are in Rome,' Syl shrug.

'What part of India do you come from?'

'West India.'

'What is your name?'

'Ram Singh Ali Mohommed – Esquire,' Syl say.

'I don't know,' the Englisher hedging. 'What are you a student of?'

'I am a student of life,' Syl say stoutly, and add, for good measure, 'are we not all?'

Same time, as the two of them stand there talking, a Indian tenant come to go inside. This test have a big beard and he wearing turban.

'*Acha, bhai,*' he say gravely to Syl, and at the same time he clasp his hands together across his chest.

'Er—acha, acha,' Syl say, and then remembering some of them Indian dishes he see in restaurant, 'aloo, vindallo, dansak and chutney.'

The fellar give Syl a funny look and went inside.

Well this English landlord give Syl a room, but Syl like he living on hot coals, having to hide from this other Indian fellar (who also say his name is Ram) every time he see him, in case he start up with some kia-san-hai talk. In fact this Ram looking at Syl so suspicious that Syl feel he had to do something about it.

One evening Syl went down to the landlord and say, 'This chap Ram, I don't believe he is from India at all.'

'What do you mean?' the landlord say. 'He is a good tenant, he has been with me some months now.'

'I am from the Orient,' Syl say, 'and I can tell a pretender when I see one. In the first place he does not sleep with his head to the East. And another thing is he is always chanting in his room and creating a nuisance to the other tenants.'

'I will have to do something then,' the Englisher say.

'You don't want to cause discomfort to all the others because of one man,' Syl say.

'Quite so,' the landlord say, 'thank you for telling me.'

'Not at all,' Syl say, 'I like it here.'

And with that Syl relax, because he had no doubt the landlord would cant this Ram out of the house, and he would be able to settle down in peace.

But bam! a few evenings later, as Syl sitting down on the bed, he hear a knocking at the door.

'Just a minute,' Syl say, and run in the corner and stand up on his head. 'You can come in now,' he say.

The landlord come in. 'What are you doing?' he ask.

'I am practising my yoghourt,' Syl say.

'I have had a word with Mr Ram,' the Englisher say, 'and now it is obvious you are the one who is not from India.'

Syl come off his head and stand on his feet. 'Are you talking about Mother India?' he say.

'No,' the landlord say, 'I am talking about you having a week's notice. You are flying under false colours, you are from the West Indies. I cannot stand those immigrants, I am sorry to say.'

'You are looking at me,' Syl say, 'a born Indian who grew up on the banks of the Ganges and worked on the rice and tea plantations, and calling me a West Indian?'

'Yes,' the landlord say. 'You look like an Indian, but you are from the same islands as those immigrants. You will have to go.'

'Oh God, places so hard to get.' Syl revert back to West Indian talk. 'You can't give me a chance?'

'I am sorry,' the landlord say. 'Mr Ram has confirmed that you are not from the East.'

'I used to live in the East End,' Syl say hopefully.

'That is not far enough East,' the Englisher say. 'Take a week's notice as from today.'

Well, a week later Syl chance to meet Battersby and give him the story. 'If it wasn't for that damn Ram, he say, 'a man would of still had a place to live.'

'Wait a minute,' Bat say, 'is a fellar with a big beard, and he always wearing a turban?'

'That is the scamp,' Syl say.

'Man,' Bat say, 'that is a fellar from Jamaica what I send to the same house for a room!'

Samuel Selvon *The Housing Lark*

Coco

Coco was fourteen and alcoholic. If he were turned loose with a dollar he would find someone to buy him a gallon of Bowery wine and he would get stoned. If someone gave him pills, he would take pills. If he could get grass, he would smoke. Anything, then, but dope. After all, he said, 'I'm only fourteen.'

He was wandering around the streets one night when I met him and took him home. No one was looking for him. His mother regularly locked him out of her apartment when she was entertaining or just felt like not being bothered and Coco often spent nights just wandering around the streets, sleeping, finally, in a boiler room, a hallway or with some compassionate stranger. Anyway, no one was looking for him tonight or any night.

He stayed for nearly a year, becoming part of our family, sharing with us his warmth and insights and his problems.

He couldn't read. He couldn't tell time. He didn't know the alphabet. The only thing he knew for sure was his first and last name, and he couldn't spell them. And he had spent seven years of his life supporting the New York public schools.

He couldn't see very well. The doctor we had examine him said that his was the first case of rickets he had ever seen. Coco's chest was concave. He never wanted to go to gym because he felt like a freak. But they made him go anyway and no one ever listened. He kept running away from school. No one knew why. His teacher told me he was a 'non-intellectual' and seemed satisfied with that.

And he drank. Whenever he could he drank. Sometimes we managed to get him to go for as long as two weeks without being drunk, but then he'd see his mother in the street, she'd slip him a couple of words of discouragement and he'd be off and drinking. We tried not to get into the game, the alcoholic game that needs persecutors and good guys and guilt. We tried to make the rules clear and the rewards and punishments strong. And as long as he could put mama out of his head, he'd be okay.

But he was fourteen, and mama was still important, and we knew that we were just making the fuse a little longer, day by day a little longer, and we knew that that was all we could do.

A social worker from the welfare department came to call. It seemed that they were going to cut his mother's welfare because he wasn't living with her and she had told them to get him back with her so she could get her full allotment. Coco said no, he didn't want to go because she just drank up the money and he had no one to take care of him. The social worker suggested that he be put in a 'protective environment' for his 'own good'. I asked her what she had in mind. And what she had in mind was the state mental hospital. In any case, she said, he couldn't go on with us. It was either back to his mama for the welfare money or into the state hospital. She left him with that decision.

Our fuse extending had come as far as it could. The bomb went off. Coco disappeared. We got a call the next night that he was drunk and in the street a few blocks away. I went to get him. When I came he was lying in the gutter. He was covered with dirt from his head to his feet. He was crying.

'I'm sorry Larry, I'm sorry,' he kept saying and then pounded his fist or his head or his body into whatever he could for punctuation of his guilt and unhappiness.

'C'mon man, Coco,' I said, 'c'mon home.'

He swung at me. He swung at me a lot, but somehow never hit me. We wrestled a lot, and I knew that was for hugging and being hugged and, occasionally, a test of strength. I always won. He was big and strong for his age, and sometimes I think he let me win.

'C'mon Coco, c'mon Coco man, let's go home,' I tried again.

'I ain't goin' to no fuckin' hospital,' he cried.

'I know you ain't,' I said, and took him home.

The city forgot about him for a while, and we put Coco into a special reading school at NYU. He went every day and was starving to learn. He wasn't drinking. He slept with his books.

Two weeks later NYU dismissed him. It seems you have to read at least third-grade level to make it there. He was off the scale. So they kicked him out. We got him a tutor.

His tutor's name was Bob Bosworth and he was the best man in a one-to-one thing with a kid I have ever seen. He was gentle and he was solid. He taught Coco to read by walking with him and reading street signs. They stopped for coffee and the menu became reading text. They read the signs on the side of buses. Telephone booths. Movies, taxicabs, police phones, butcher shops, supermarkets, candy stores, liquor stores even. When Coco slept late, which wasn't often, Bob would go up to his room and wake him. Slowly, Coco got on the reading scale. He learned to write his name. He learned the alphabet. When we went out in the car he read every sign he could get. In the restaurants he would study the menu carefully.

'H-a-m and c-h-e-e-s-e – that's ham and cheese,' he would say proudly and loudly. Very loudly.

And sometimes he would say ham and cheese when it read ham and swiss, but more often than not, he got it right on the nose. Other times he would test to make sure we were listening. Then when he saw we were, he would smile.

His drinking episodes were getting further and further apart.

By the time Coco was fifteen he was talking about going back into some kind of school. He was physically well, his feelings about himself had moved upward somewhat from zero, and he laughed a lot. Michelle had taken fifteen minutes a night for one week and taught him how to tell time and he wore a watch, offering the time to anyone he thought might be a little off schedule. I remember thinking that of all the changes he went through in the three years I had known him, the most important to him was that he could tell time.

His mother, in the meanwhile, had moved from place to place and for some time Coco couldn't find her. At one point he heard she went to Puerto Rico and that made him happy because there she would be with family. He talked about her more and more and the talk was warm and loving. He understood why she drank a lot and why it was hard for her to take care of him, he said, 'It's hard to have kids by yourself.'

When his mother returned to the scene, the social worker materialized with her.

'Coco will just have to go home,' she said, 'after all, she is his mother.'

'Where has she been for the last year and a half?' I asked, not wanting to challenge her motherhood as much as her motives. 'You know, no one's taken care of this kid since he was a baby?'

I heard both what I was saying and more. What had begun as a desperate move had become a tremendous investment. Coco had really become part of us and I was being bitchy about his mother. And resentful. I had done what all the books said not to do. I had gotten involved with a lost kid who needed some love.

But the fact of birth is incontestable. For whatever reasons she wanted him back with her, whatever her sins of neglect or indifference had been, she was Coco's mother. He knew it and we knew it.

So one day, just as he had come, Coco left without saying goodbye.

For a few months, as hard as we looked to spot him around the neighbourhood we couldn't find him. His mother lived nearby and no one was ever home. Coco just disappeared.

More than a year went by, I heard that Coco was back on the bottle, but I never saw him. Kids said he was in pretty bad shape but that he wasn't around much. He was spending a lot of time in Brooklyn. Some thought he might have put himself in the hospital. We couldn't find out.

One night nearly three years after the social worker sent Coco home the buzzer buzzed and I went to the window to see who it was. It was Coco and he was drunk. He was banging on the front door of our building and our landlady was screaming at him to stop or she would call the police. Infuriated, he was trying to break down the door as I came down.

I opened the door and went out to him. He was really torn up. He was much bigger than the last time I had seen him. He was already eighteen. His eyes were glassy as if he had taken a lot of pills with his wine.

'Larry, man . . .' he said, barely able to stand on his own.

'Larry man, I'm a junkie. A goddam junkie. Look at me man. I'm all fucked up.'

I sat down on the stoop with him and put my arm around him. We cried a little, but he was too stoned to talk to. He just wanted to talk and he came to do that.

'Remember Bob Bosworth?' he asked, reeling and not waiting for an answer.

'He really gave a shit about me.'

'Yeah. He did,' I said.

'Y'know, I wish I could go back and do that again. That was the bestest time in my life. That Bosworth, man, he sure could teach.'

The message was delivered. Coco got up and smiled and walked away. I watched him stumble down the street and around the corner.

Larry Coles

EH 14

Limitations

Lana Webb: aged twenty-three

Could Lana be spoken to? Yes, apparently, provided that one did not demand an answer. She belongs to the village and she is emphatically not a recluse. If folk avoid her, that is their look out! She makes it plain that she had not withdrawn from life, complicated though life may be. She is here, smooth and still, washed and tidy, decent enough for anybody who might drop in. Her name is written in as many different places as that of anyone else, the chapel register, the school attendance book, the electoral roll, at the newsagents (*Secrets*, *Honey*, *Lucky Star*, *True Romance* – she is a great reader and is known for always having her nose stuck in a book) and at the National Assistance Board. Everybody in Akenfield knows Lana and if they don't come to see her, 'Well, that's their loss!' laughs her Gran. The joke is a good one and momentarily engulfs them both. They emerge from it like divers from a pool, shaking their heads and dashing moisture from their eyes with the backs of hands.

'You're lucky that it's only your eyes that are running!' says Lana.

Gran turns away with a 'hoop-hoop!' Her shoulders shake. 'Now don't start me off again, there's a good girl,' she says.

They both have to raise their voices in order to be heard above the crackling pop coming through the fretwork sunburst of a thirties wireless. The lino is translucent, like sucked toffee, its pattern all licked off by the duster. Shining ornaments, shining blacklead, shining skin on Lana's strong bare legs hanging out of their mini-skirt. Regularly, and much louder than anything else, there is the dungeon-like rattle of a chain being wearily dragged in and out of a barrel. It is Terry, Gran's dog. He is a collie aged thirteen with fat dusty haunches and golden eyes which need wiping. He was fastened to the barrel when he was one and has never been unfastened since. 'Terry!' calls Gran. 'He has what we have – don't you, boy?' 'Good boy!' shouts Lana.

The cottage is partly a soldier's resettlement hut of the First World War and partly a railway carriage, and is quite inordinately pretty. The two units are set in an L and the join is covered with house-leeks and stone-crop, cushions of grass and Paul Scarlet roses. Brass carriage handles glitter behind leaves. Little paths maze around and are edged with beer bottles, their necks driven into the earth. It is a toy house for playing mothers-and-fathers in. Except that the fathers, big, clumsy, nasty things, have long since been ousted from the game. Their speckled photographs glare down from the walls. Both dad and grandad have been dead for years – 'Why, you hardly knew your dad, did you, Larn?' cries Gran with relief. 'Now my husband,' she points to a boy-scout with his hat set on a bamboo table like a meal, 'he lasted for a long time'. Her eyes show patience, resignation, God's will being done.

Lana glances guiltily at the pictures because of Ken. He is in her handbag, along with a facsimiled autographed photo of Ringo Starr, her birth certificate and her horoscope. But somehow there is no need to fret about Ken, who is a kind, stout man of perhaps thirty-eight with his pockets stretched out with Bibles, and change for his insurance round. Ken has known Lana since she was twelve. 'And it shows the kind of chap he is that it never made a scrap of difference to his feelings for her,' says Gran.

Lana prinks in the armchair in which she has been sitting all this time and there is a distinct flap and squeak of drenched rubber.

'The doctor himself said it was nothing to be ashamed of,' declares Gran.

'Of course not!' one agrees in a fiercely 'civilized' voice.

Gran and Lana's eyes meet in wordless discussion. Yes? Yes. Gran goes to a cream-painted door and opens it with a flourish in which candour competes with pride. There is evidently another addition to the toy house which cannot be seen from the road and which makes it an F, not an L. It is a long white room with windows open on either side, and the wind hurtles through it. It is blowing some twenty pairs of knickers. Pink, white, blue, flowered, plain, nylon, cotton, they jig happily above a galvanized zinc bath in which sheets are steeping. Gran closes the door and Lana, her expression faintly amused and challenging now, rises from her chair and goes off somewhere to change. The movement causes an odd Alice-like transformation. Sitting, she is a slumped odalisque. Standing, she is a very big little girl. The door of the second-class compartment clicks behind her.

'You should just see her room,' says Gran. 'Like a princess's, and she does it all herself. Of course, it hasn't been all honey. It's been a struggle, I can tell you. Only He knows. But neither of us would say thank you to a change now. What with my bit of pension and her bit of National, we're quids in.'

Lana's past is as much an open book as her present. Her father was an American, her mother Gran's daughter. The daughter was known as a 'good girl' and had thus been tricked, bewitched or raped by the American. But it all worked out for the best and from the time Lana went to school until her mother's death from a heart attack when the child was fourteen they were 'all in all to each other'. Lana didn't have children as friends; there was no need. She had Mum, who walked her to and from school until the day she left. She slept with Mum in the second-class compartment and it was in this room, with 'Smoking' frosted on the windows, that Mum cut out and made all Lana's clothes from give-away patterns in the women's magazines. Every Saturday night Ken arrived in his black-japanned Morris and drove them to his Mum's in Ipswich, where they watched television. Gran now went on this outing with Lana, who sat on a pile of *Daily Expresses* which Ken provided. The whole village agreed that Ken had been wonderful.

Lana had wetted the bed as a child, of course, said Gran. But you couldn't call that Incontinence, could you? This had begun six years ago and Lana hadn't been dry since. 'Wet as a ditch, day in, day out.' She got through fifteen pairs of knickers a day, not to mention all her bed-linen.

And pads *and* rubbers and anything you like to mention. She had had two operations and they had made her worse (Triumph). She don't feel a thing.

Lana returned to her chair at this point. Did she knit, perhaps? Do anything? 'Glory, no!' laughs Gran. Both shook with merriment at the very idea. 'You see,' explained Gran, 'Incontinence is a way of life. Those were the doctor's very words, weren't they, Larn? She can't go to the pictures, not to the chapel, nor nowhere.'

'And Ken?'

'Ken's got his Mum, hasn't he?'

Gran picks up a jug and begins to water her pot-plants. A swing-wing bomber from Bentwaters knifes up the iridescent Akenfield afternoon, its scream momentarily and intolerably trapped in the cottage.

'Blessed Yanks!' says Gran – 'If ever I should swear!'

Ronald Blythe *Akenfield: Portrait of an English Village*

The Threepenny Tip

It was near the end of the round. I leant the old paper-bike against the house wall and went round the back. It was a typical council house. The back fence hadn't seen creosote in years. I knocked on the tall gate. The dog inside started barking.

'Coming! Shut up, Rusty! Get down!'

The old woman opened the gate.

'Cold morning, isn't it?' I said.

'Yes,' she sighed. She shut the gate.

The yard wasn't big, so the dog was always trying to get out. They had built a rough old shed next to the outside toilet. They used it for the dog's kennel and to keep the old man's wheelchair dry.

We went in the kitchen. It stunk of the Sunday dinner. It was a small, dank kitchen. An old, large, enamelled gas stove boiled something on the top in an old brown saucepan. She opened another door and we went into the living room. The old man, as usual, was sitting in front of the fire. I handed him his *Sunday Mirror*.

'Got any shillings this week, luv?' she asked.

'Yes, I think so.' I gave her the *News of The World* and emptied my money on the grubby-white tablecloth. She paid for the papers and slipped a threepenny bit over to me. I looked her in the eyes, as if to say no thank you. She passed me a ten-shilling note. I gave her ten shilling pieces.

'Thank you,' she said and put them in her purse.

I put my money back into the bag. She spent most of her money on keeping the house warm. If her husband got cold, it would make him cough. He had progressive lung cancer.

I gazed around the living room as she spoke. The mantlepiece was an array of pictures and ornaments. In the middle was an old clock with Roman pillars and a pediment over the top. It didn't go, it was stuck on ten past three. The battered settee, with newspaper on the seats, was in front of the fire. The old man always sat there. Behind him was the sideboard. This, too, was covered in pictures and curios and another clock. This one did work, but was always five minutes fast. I glanced down at the floor; it had a grubby, brown carpet, well-worn, no doubt a wedding present. The room smelt of the cooking in the kitchen. It lingered about and smeared the windows. As I sat at the table opposite the window, I noticed the crumbs on the tablecloth which had been left over from breakfast.

The old man put on his glasses. He never said much. I'd say he was about seventy-one. I could only guess on his height, as I had never seen him standing up. I knew he could hardly walk, though he always had a walking stick near him. He wore the same scrubby, black jacket and cap all the time. He always wore a shirt without a collar. I think he did this so as to breath easier. He was virtually bald, but he had a few strands of white hair. He wore a small moustache, which covered a part of that face. It was blotchy and heavily wrinkled. His giant eyes loomed up through his extra-strong glasses. He held his paper in his large, weak hands. He started coughing and wheezing. His wife stopped talking for a moment. Then started again. The old man was a pathetic wreck. I just had to look away from him.

There were many times I wish, I wished I'd had not been there. The old man could not use the outside toilet. So, being poor, he used a jam jar in his lap. For weeks, I wondered why he used to groan and flinch when he had a towel on his lap. He was embarrased and hurt when I noticed. It was as bad as the time when he tried to get up and reach the paper and fell down.

The mongrel dog jumped up.

'Get down, Rusty!' shouted the old woman. The old man said something too, but I couldn't understand what he said. Each week he used to cough more often and the nurse came more often, too. He began to lose weight.

His cheeks fell in. His face became hideous. The coughing fits lasted longer and they were terrible to listen to. I found that I was glad to get away. Then, one week, when I went in, he was not there.

'Where's the old . . . er, your husband?'

'He. . . .' She broke off and looked at the settee. 'He died on Thursday.'

I couldn't speak, even if I'd wanted to.

'*News of The World* only, please.' She gave me the money. I put it in my bag. 'Any shilli . . .'

'No shillings,' she said.

Then she handed me that threepenny tip.

I could have cried.

Mark Maplethorpe *aged 16*

Seeing the Doctor

Only her feet betray her. There is something about the way she walks on her feet – a kind of irresponsibility towards them – which is still quite childish. Her figure is 36-25-36.

She was crying when she came into thc surgery.

'What's wrong Duckie?'

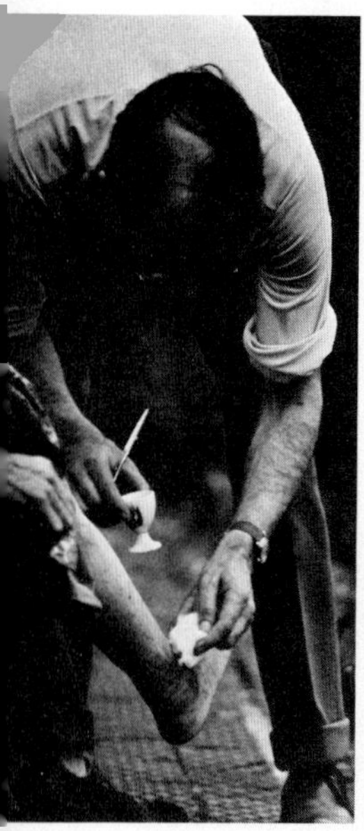

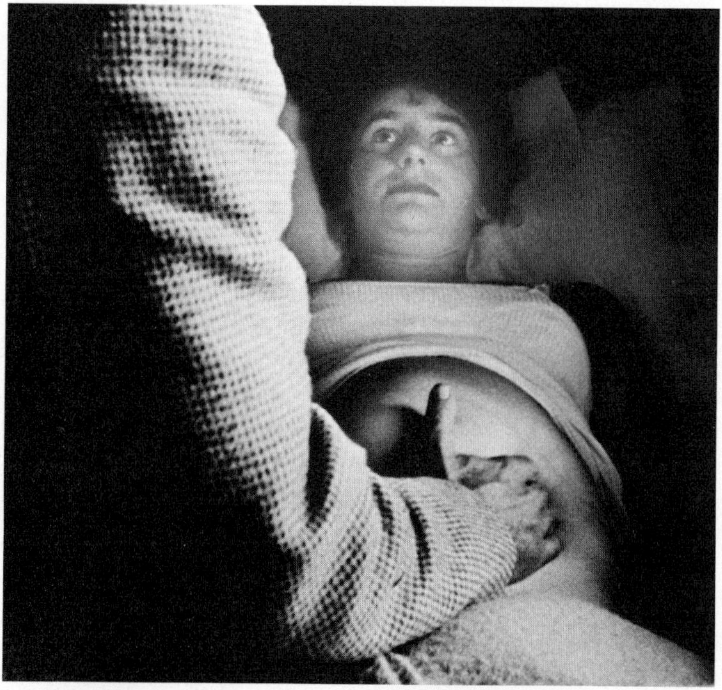

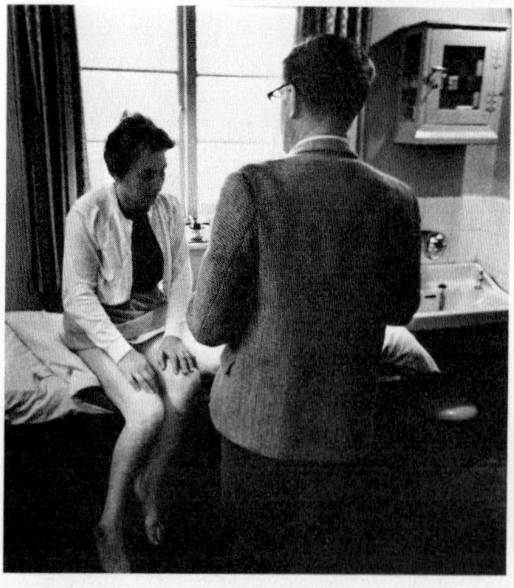

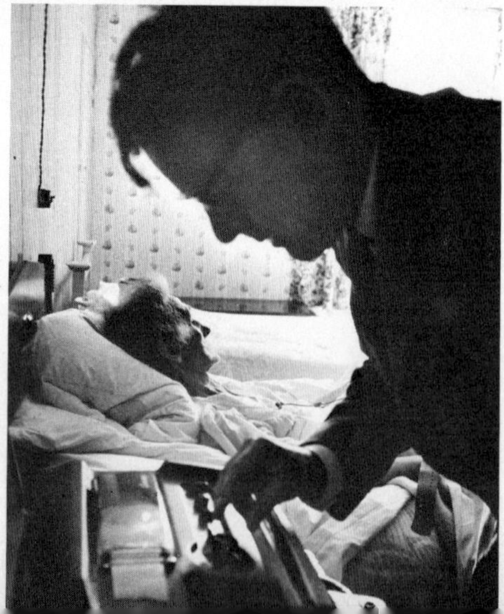

'I just feel sort of miserable.'

She sat like other girls had sat there crying because they thought they were pregnant. To make it easier for her, the doctor slipped the question between several others.

'What's getting you down?'

No answer.

'Sore throat?'

'Not now.'

'Water-works all right?'

She nodded.

'Have you got a temperature?'

She shook her head.

'Periods regular?'

'Yeah.'

'When was your last one?'

'Last week.'

The doctor paused.

'Do you remember that rash you used to get on your tum? Has it ever come back?'

'No.'

He leant forward in his chair towards her.

'You just feel weepy?'

She inclined her head farther towards her own consoling bosom.

'Did Mum and Dad put you up to come to me?'

'No, I came myself.'

'Even having your hair dyed didn't make you feel better?'

She laughed a little because he had noticed. 'It did for a while.'

The doctor took her temperature, looked at her throat and told her to stay in bed for two days. Then resumed the conversation.

'Do you like working in that laundry?'

'It's a job.'

'What about the other girls there?'

'I don't know.'

'Do you get on with them?'

'You get stopped if they find you talking.'

'Have you thought of doing anything else?'

'What can I do?'

'What would you like to do?'

'I'd like to do secretarial work.'

'Who would you like to be secretary to?'

She laughed and shook her head.

Her face was grubby with tear stains. But around her eyes and in the muzzle of her face which terminates in her full lip-sticked lips there is evidence of the same force that has filled out her bust and hips. She is nubile in everything except her education and her chances.

'When you're a bit better I'll keep you off work for a few days, if you like, and you can go to the Labour Exchange and find out how you can get trained. There are all kinds of training schemes.'

'Are there?' she said moodily.

'How did you do at school?'

'I wasn't any good.'

'Did you take O-levels?'

'No, I left.'

'But you weren't stupid were you?' He asked this as though if she admitted that she was, it would somehow reflect badly on him.

'No, not stupid.'

'Well,' he said.

'It's terrible that laundry. I hate it.'

'It's no good being sorry for yourself. If I give you a week off, will you really use it?'

She nodded, chewing her damp handkerchief.

'You can come up again on Wednesday and I'll phone the Labour Exchange and we'll talk about what they say.'

'I'm sorry,' she said, beginning to cry again.

'Don't be sorry. The fact that you're crying means that you've got imagination. If you didn't have imagination, you wouldn't feel so bad. Now go to bed and stay there tomorrow.'

Through the surgery window he saw her walking up the lane to the common, to the house in which he had delivered her sixteen years ago. After she had turned the corner, he continued to stare at the stone walls on either side of the lane. Once they were dry walls. Now their stones were cemented together.

John Berger *A Fortunate Man*

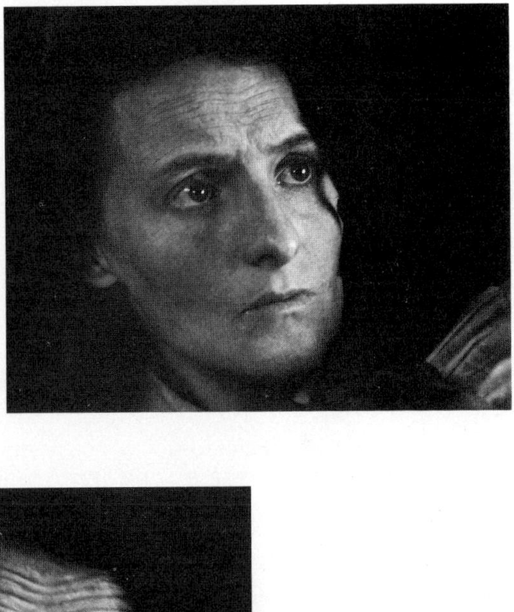

Where I Live

Once he was putting a syringe deep into a
man's chest; there was little question of pain
but it made the man feel bad: the man tried
to explain his revulsion: 'That's where I live,
where you're putting that needle in.'

'I know,' Sassall said, 'I know what it feels like.
I can't bear anything done near my eyes,
I can't bear to be touched there.
I think that's where I live,
just under and behind my eyes.'

John Berger *A Fortunate Man*

Suffering

Ugly creatures, ugly grunting creatures,
Completely concealed under the point of the needle,
  behind the curve of the Research Task Graph,
Disgusting creatures with foam at the mouth,
  with bristles on their bottoms,
One after the other
They close their pink mouths

They open their pink mouths
They grow pale
Flutter their legs
  as if they were running a very
  long distance,

They close ugly blue eyes,
They open ugly blue eyes
  and
  they're
  dead.

But I ask no questions,
  no one asks any questions.

And after their death we let the ugly creatures
  run in pieces along the white expanse
  of the paper electrophore
We let them graze in the greenish-blue pool
  of the chromatogram
And in pieces we drive them for a dip
  in alcohol
  and xylol
And the immense eye of the ugly animal god
  watches their every move
  through the tube of the microscope
And the bits of animals are satisfied
  like flowers in a flower-pot
  like kittens at the bottom of a pond
  like cells before conception.
But I ask no questions,
  no one asks any questions,
Naturally no one asks
Whether these creatures wouldn't have preferred
  to live all in one piece,
  their disgusting life
  in bogs
  and canals,
Whether they wouldn't have preferred to eat
  one another alive,
Whether they wouldn't have preferred to make love
  in between horror and hunger,

Whether they wouldn't have preferred to use
   all their eyes and pores to perceive
   their muddy stinking little world
Incredibly terrified,
Incredibly happy
In the way of matter which can do no more.

But I ask no questions,
   no one asks any questions,
Because it's all quite useless,
Experiments succeed and experiments fail,
Like everything else in this world,
   in which the truth advances
   like some splendid silver bulldozer
   in the tumbling darkness,

Like everything else in this world,
   in which I met a lonely girl
   inside a shop selling bridal veils,
In which I met a general covered
   with oak leaves,
In which I met ambulance men who could find no
   wounded,
In which I met a man who had lost
   his name,
In which I met a glorious and famous, bronze,
   incredibly terrified rat,
In which I met people who wanted to lay down
   their lives and people who wanted to lay down
   their heads in sorrow,
In which, come to think of it, I keep meeting my
   own self at every step.

Miroslav Holub *Translated from the Czech by George Theiner*

Plague Burial

When the eagerly expected warmer weather came at last, it brought along a plague. The people whom it struck wriggled with pain, were shaken by a ghastly chill, and died without regaining consciousness. I rushed with Olga from hut to hut, stared at the patients in order to drive the sickness out of them, but all to no avail. The disease proved too strong. Behind the tightly shut windows, inside the half-dark huts, the dying and suffering groaned and cried out. The plague persisted.

One evening my face began to burn and I shook with uncontrollable tremors. Olga looked for a moment into my eyes and placed her cold hand on my brow. Then rapidly and wordlessly she dragged me toward a distant field. There she dug a deep pit and ordered me to jump in.

While I stood at the bottom, trembling with fever and chill, Olga pushed the earth back into the pit until I was buried up to my neck. Then she trampled the soil around me and beat it with the shovel until the surface was very smooth. After making sure there were no anthills in the vicinity, she made three smoky fires of peat.

Thus planted in the cold earth, my body cooled completely in a few moments, like the root of a wilting weed. I lost all awareness. Like an abandoned head of cabbage, I became part of the great field.

Olga did not forget me. Several times during the day she brought cool drinks which she poured into my mouth and which seemed to drain right through my body into the earth. The smoke from the fires, which she stoked with fresh moss, misted my eyes and stung my throat. Seen from the earth's surface when the wind occasionally cleared the smoke away, the world looked like a rough rug. The small plants growing round about loomed as tall as trees. The figure of Olga approaching cast a shadow like an unearthly giant's over the landscape.

Having fed me at twilight for the last time, she threw fresh peat on the fires and went to her hut to sleep. I remained in the field, alone, rooted into the earth which seemed to draw me down deeper and deeper.

At times, feeling the wind on my brow, I went numb with horror. In my imagination I saw armies of ants and cockroaches calling to one another and scurrying toward my head, to some place under the top of my skull, where they would build new nests. There they would eat out my thoughts, one after another, until I would become as empty as the shell of a pumpkin from which all the fruit has been scraped out.

Noises woke me. I opened my eyes, uncertain of my surroundings. I was fused with the earth, but thoughts stirred in my heavy head. The world was greying. The fires had gone out. On my lips I felt the cold of streaming dew. Drops of it settled on my face and in my hair.

The sounds returned. A flock of ravens circled over my head. One of them landed nearby on broad, rustling wings. It approached my head while the others began to alight.

In terror I watched their shining, black-feathered tails and darting eyes. They stalked around me, nearer and nearer, flicking their heads toward me, uncertain whether I was dead or alive.

I did not wait for what would come next. I screamed. The startled ravens leapt back. Several rose a few feet into the air, but touched ground again not far off. Then they glanced suspiciously at me and began their circuitous march.

I shouted once more. But this time they were not frightened, and with increasing boldness approached ever more closely. My heart thudded. I did not know what to do. I screamed again but now the birds showed no fear. They were not two feet from me. Their shapes loomed larger in my eyes, their beaks grew more and more vicious. The curved, widespread claws of their feet resembled huge rakes.

One of the ravens halted in front of me, inches from my nose. I yelled right into its face, but the raven only gave a slight jerk and opened its beak. Before I could shout again, it pecked at my head and several of my hairs appeared in its mouth. The bird struck again, tearing out another tuft of hair. I turned my head from side to side, loosening the earth around my neck. But my movements only made the birds more curious. They surrounded me and pecked at me wherever they could. I began to scream loudly, but my voice was too weak to rise above the earth and only seeped back into the soil without reaching the hut where Olga lay.

The birds played with me freely. The more furiously I swivelled my head to and fro, the more excited and bold they became. Seeming to avoid my face, they attacked the hair at the back of my head.

My strength ebbed. To move my head each time seemed like shifting a huge sack of grain from one place to another. I was crazed and saw everything as through a fog.

I gave up. I was myself now a bird. I was trying to free my chilled wings from the earth. Stretching my limbs, I joined the flock of ravens.

Olga found me in the midst of the swarming flock of ravens. I was nearly frozen and my head was deeply lacerated by the birds. She quickly dug me out.

After several days my health returned. Olga said that the cold earth had driven the sickness out of me. She said that the disease was picked up by a throng of ghosts transformed into ravens which tasted my blood to make sure that I was one of them. This was the only reason, she asserted, they did not peck my eyes out.

Jerzy Kosinski

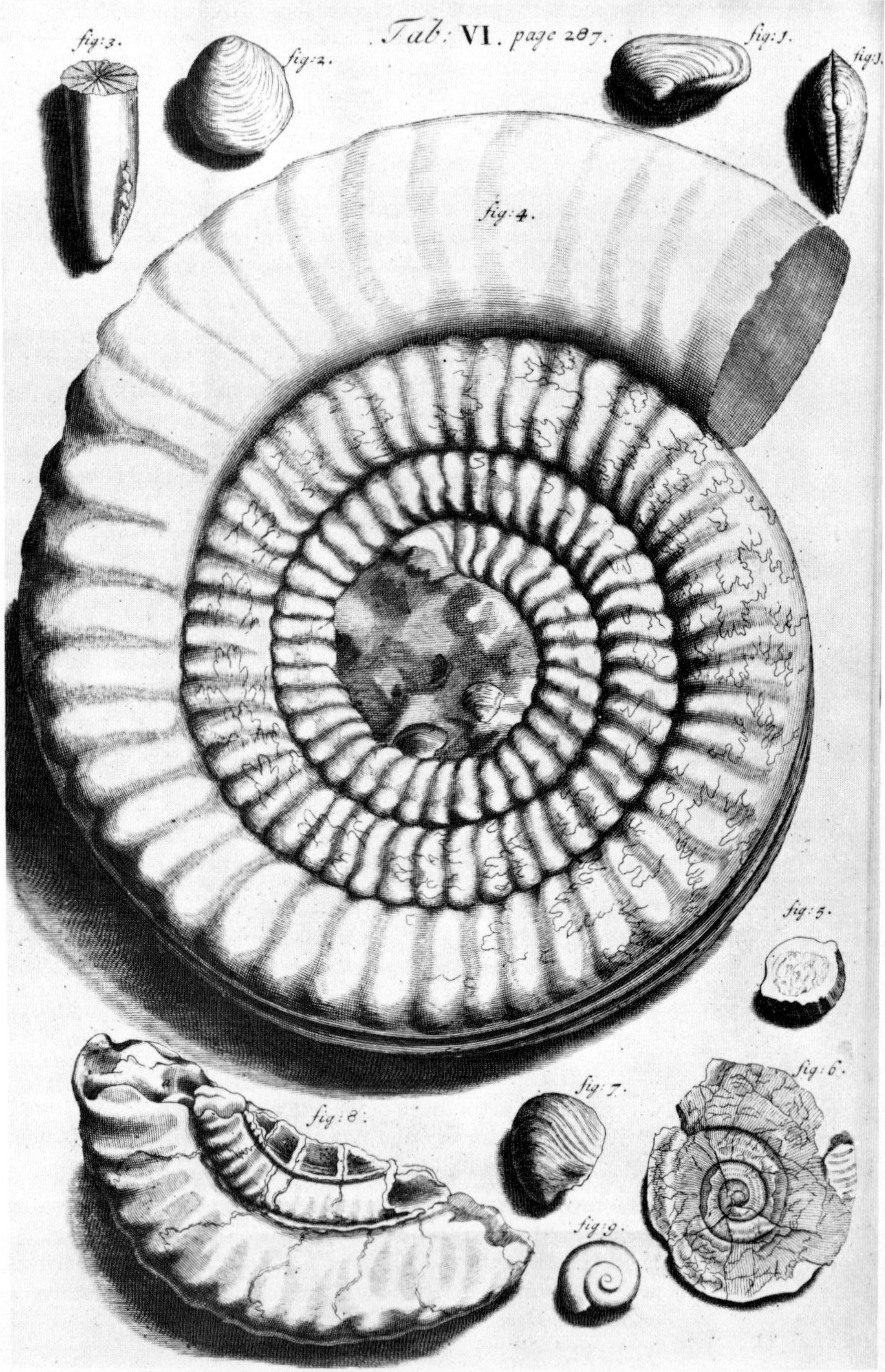
Tab: VI. page 287.
fig: 3.
fig: 2.
fig: 1.
fig: 4.
fig: 5.
fig: 6.
fig: 7.
fig: 8.
fig: 9.

A Genuine Illumination

At this ungainly moment of my life it would have occurred to nobody, and least of all to me, that on the very next day I was to see a great light. It happened on a run. The weather was so bad at the beginning of that term that cricket was impossible, so after lunch, we all sloshed off in the rain in a straggling column across country, shepherded by Mr Johnson, the music master, an unhappy intellectual to whom these chores fell as if by some natural law. After about a mile and a half I was leaning against a gate between two sodden lengths of cow pasture, getting my breath back, when I suddenly saw in the scuffed mud patch under the gate a piece of stone washed clear by the rain, and, contained in it, an intricate and perfect ribbed coil, like a coiled up snake, in a sort of dull gold. It was a beautiful object and a splendid find, and I was just wondering whether I could possibly carry it back, or should I hide it somewhere to be recovered on Sunday when I didn't have to run, when Mr Johnson appeared, more than inclined to lean on the same gate and get his breath back.

'Oh, sir,' I said, 'what's this?'

'That's an ammonite,' said Mr Johnson, puffing and blowing, 'a fossil shell, very old, used to live here when all this land was under the sea a long time ago.'

'Before the Romans and Ancient Britons?' I asked.

'Oh, long before, about sixty million years ago, before there were any men at all,' he said. 'At least, I think that's right, they seem to change the estimate about every five years.'

'Sixty million years old? Before or after the world was made in six days?'

'Well, metaphorically,' Mr Johnson said, 'about the Thursday of that week. An interesting period geologically: the giant lizards, the dinosaurs, the first flying beasts, the pterodactyls – they're all here still under the ground. This part of England is full of them.

I don't know why this revelation of the huge continuity of the past should have been such a release to my imagination, but it was. It was a genuine illumination – somethimg to do with perspective, something to do with the mysterious quality of time itself. Something to do with buried treasure, something which joined the separate worlds of poetry and finding out and learning and digging and the splendid look of the country. Something which put cricket in its pettifogging place. During that summer term, I rarely emerged from the Jurassic Age. I found a quarry full of ammonites and belemnites and terebratulae and rhynconellae and gryphaea and pecten and sea urchins. A whole sea bottom of creatures who'd lived and died and left themselves to be explained – this was the point – before anyone could possibly have explained them. With great difficulty I read that holy book *The Origin of Species*. I sent for everything that the South Kensington Museum had published about the Jurassic and Lower Lias. I knew the names of all the creatures. The greatest day was when I found among the sharks' teeth in the blue clay the perfect imprint of a fish nearly two feet long.

I found my fish about four o'clock on a July afternoon. On a Sunday of course. At nine o'clock by the stable clock that morning I put my name down to be absent from lunch and drew my sandwiches from the pantry, shouldered my haversack and builder's trowel and square-faced hammer, and set off down the chestnut avenue where all the bees were buzzing, and where the white dust of the roads of those days lay thick enough to mute my footsteps and rise up in puffs of smoke when I ran.

I turned right over a stile and illegally along the edge of a hayfield, waist-deep in the hot, scented, multi-coloured mixture of grasses and weeds, and over the railway embankment, climbing down the long moraine of rocks which drained it and reinforced it, up the other side, down the side of the big barley field, waving like a sand-coloured sea, and on downhill to a meadow badly farmed and full of ragwort under whose harsh yellow flowers you could find millions of the black and yellow caterpillars which turned into Cinnabar moths, and over another stile into a sort of wilderness of long grass through which wound the brook in its own canyon about ten feet deep and twenty feet wide. The water was low and the biggest pool not ten feet wide or three feet deep. Long bone-coloured grasses grew on the tops of little cliffs and rushes and yellow flags at the water's edge. I heard the birds signal my arrival and then stop and fall very silent. There was a swishing noise of a cow eating grass on the cliff top. Bright blue and bright yellow little dragonflies flicked about like neon signs over the water and a water rat, not quite silently, slid under and was off. I took off my shirt. The summer's geology had burnt me a toast colour. I took off my shoes and put my feet in the water and just sat for ten minutes, possessing my estate – this fifty yards of brook. In the glare of the sun, eyes slightly unfocused, the yellows and tans and off-whites of the dried grasses and the coins of sunlight on the water splintered and disintegrated into zig-zags of light as in a picture by Van Gogh. Everything went a little darker and the insect hum became more important. Some small degree of self-hypnosis and sun-drunkenness was an integral part of this act of worship.

I sat very still and the birds began to regain their confidence. The cow came over to look at me, and three rabbits lolloped into view. You had to sit there until you were satisfied that you were part of all this. And then participation could move on to its next stage. The uncovering of the other world. From the edge of the stream to the foot of the taller cliff – the twelve-foot one, of cigar-coloured silt – on the floor of the canyon a strip of dark blue clay was laid bare. The Lower Lias in all its glory. When the spirit moved me, I walked across with my haversack, lay on my stomach on the grass and began to peel off with the trowel the first layer of clay. Fossils were to be found scattered all through the clay perfectly preserved, but every so often a layer of hard cemented stone occurred, a flat pavement three to six inches thick, and in and under this the life of the ancient ocean floor had become compacted and was as thick as gravel in concrete. I found one of these layers at about midday, and knocked off for my sandwiches and to take a trip down to the next bay of the stream to see the kingfisher who was streaking about as usual like blue lightning. Then I just lay in the sun and roasted and then, at about two, I got down to work. It was the richest load I had ever struck. Every layer something new, rich, strange. The heat of the afternoon was over the hill when I decided to yank out a two-foot block of it which seemed separate, before I knocked off for the day. It took me an hour to haul it out – a long, oval stone covered in hieroglyphs of shells in section and on edge and at the end something I couldn't place, a sort of wavy pattern in black and white which disappeared into the stone matrix. I took out my knife, a huge affair of many implements, and tried the biggest blade in a crack at the top of the stone. Quite suddenly it fell apart like a hinged box. There was my fish from its head to the end of its tail, which was the bit I had noticed – perfect in every scale, eyeplates, spines, teeth and the great, square, bony back plates of a shark.

I sat in the sun for half an hour or more, filled with the sense of a life made perfect, and then I emptied out my haversack, covered the contents with clay and marked the spot with a clod of earth and a stick, washed my fish gently in the stream, wrapped him in dock leaves, stowed him in the haversack and toiled up the hill. It was the last Sunday of term.

Home life was secular and distracting. There was the gramophone, the bicycle, the house in the tree, my brother John, my friend Peter, the vicar's son. I made some attempts on the local fossils, which were vegetable and carboniferous, but had to realize in the end that they wouldn't do. The deity concerned was a local god presiding over just that stretch of stream where the fish had lain so long.

The rigours of school life soon renewed the faith. In the end, it perished of its own success. The headmaster took it up. A geological society was formed. I was its secretary. I gave lectures. At one time a learned man from the South Kensington Museum came down to consult me and to take for his own glass cases a very curious shell of mine of a kind which I had never seen before. Nor, he said, had anyone else. It's somewhere in the Science Museum to this day. When, by the time of my last summer term, I had found the giant ammonites under Hallaton bridge, there were sixteen little boys digging them up and a master taking measurements. I had felt sad all day and now I suddenly knew what was wrong. I flung down my trowel in disgust. The faith had become institutionalized and I was through with it.

René Cutforth *Order to View*

Lizards and Snakes

On the summer road that ran by our front porch
Lizards and snakes came out to sun.
It was hot as a stove out there, enough to scorch
A buzzard's foot. Still, it was fun
To lie in the dust and spy on them. Near but remote,
They snoozed in the carriage ruts, a smile
In the set of the jaw, a fierce pulse in the throat
Working away like Jack Doyle's after he'd run the mile.

Aunt Martha had an unfair prejudice
Against them (as well as being cold
Towards bats). She was pretty inflexible in this,
Being a spinster and all, and old.
So we used to slip them into her knitting box.
In the evening she'd bring in things to mend
And a nice surprise would slide out from under the socks.
It broadened her life, as Joe said. Joe was my friend.

But we never did it again after the day
Of the big wind when you could hear the trees
Creak like rocking chairs. She was looking away
Off, and kept saying, 'Sweet Jesus, please
Don't let him near me. He's as like as twins.
He can crack us like lice with his fingernail.
I can see him plain as a pikestaff. Look how he grins
And swings the scaly horror of his folded tail.'

Anthony Hecht

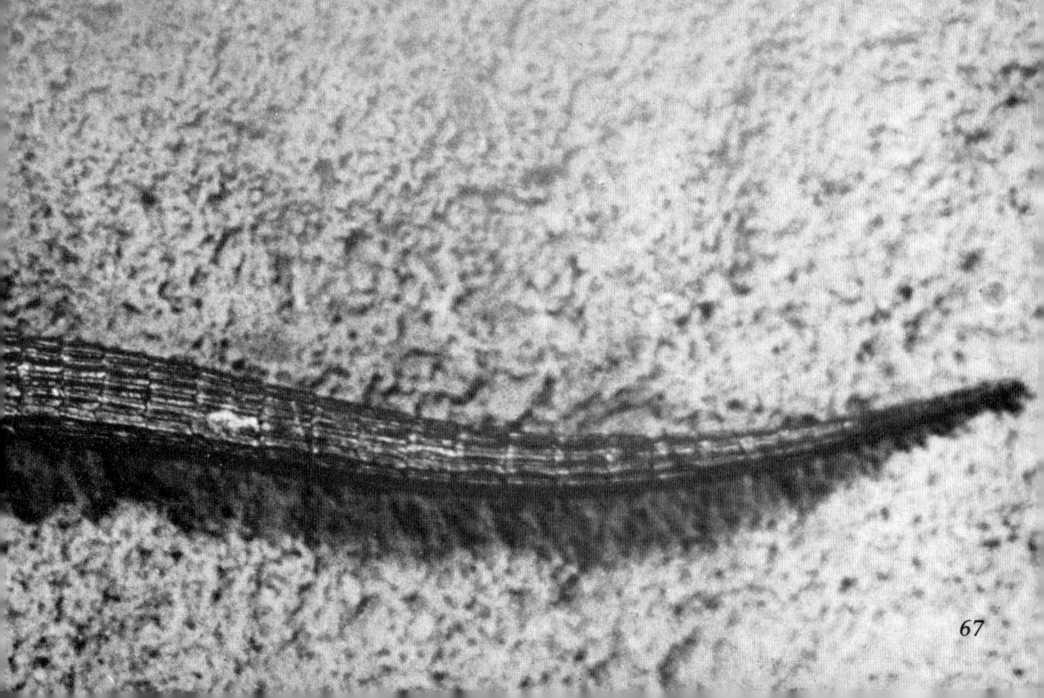

Becoming a Human Being

I probably could have heard the hoofbeats as she fled had I not fell asleep directly, there being little else in the way of wrapping so cosy as a buffalo robe when you get the hang of it. Though at first it tends to be stiff on the skinned side, whereas the hair on the other is rough as a brush, it soon cleaves to the body from your natural warmth and becomes as if you have growed it on yourself.

Next thing I knowed, that young boy Little Horse woke me up in the dawn. 'Come on,' he indicated; and shivering off the remains of my sleep, which wasn't hard to do because of the cold of that time of morning, I followed him out to the field where the ponies was pastured. There was markedly fewer than when I had seen the herd the day before: Caroline's theft of one was nothing to what some Ute had come and stole a little later on, or maybe it was the Pawnee this time. Anyway, unless Old Lodge Skin's crowd went out soon and stole some horses back, they would all be walking.

Little Horse already knowed, as an Indian would, that Caroline had run off and figured correctly that I was going to stay and be part of the tribe, having no alternative, and he had woke me to go with him because that was the duty of the boys of my age: tending the ponies

first thing every morning. Which is to say, he knew more about me than I did myself at that moment, but his grin was in no wise mocking or mean as we left the tepeeful of sleeping Cheyenne grown-ups. Indians don't rise especially early when nothing's doing, except for the boys.

Outside the dawn was blue, and chill to go with it. I hadn't had one particle of my clothes off for a couple of days, and not washed for the same space of time, enjoying my deficiency. I mention that because I recall thinking about it and feeling luxurious. Even as a small boy, a white man gets that sort of idea when he goes among Indians: What the hell does anything matter? I'm with savages, don't have to wash, can go to the toilet right where I stand, and so on. My point here is that, on the contrary, a Cheyenne takes a bath every day in the nearest water, and even if they hadn't observed that custom, there would have been another requirement to take its place. If you're a human being, you can't get away from any obligations.

On the route to the meadow, me and Little Horse encountered various other lads going to the same chore, aged eight to twelve; and on account of the thefts, there was so few ponies left that the herdsmen almost outnumbered the stock. Our job turned out to be leading the animals to the creek for watering. After which we took them to a new

pasturage, for they had ate quite a bit of grass from the old one, and after all, the plains belonged to us far as the eye could see.

Little Horse and the other boys did a lot of gassing and laughing among themselves, and for all I know it might have been at my expense. I was alone in so far as wearing pants, shirt, boots and hat; but after we rehobbled the lead mare to keep the herd from straying and went back to the creek and stripped down to take that bath I mentioned, I was distinguished only by my skin, and when we came back out of the water – which was fairly cold to start with but warmed once you were in, especially because of the horseplay that Indian boys give a lot of time to – why, I left off all my duds except the wool pants. Gave everything away, in fact, which made me a lot of immediate friends.

When we got back to the lodges, the recipients went inside and brought out Cheyenne stuff in return. That was when I finally took off the pants and got into the buckskin breechclout that one of the boys gave me, and secured it with the belt I had from another. Also put on moccasins; and received a dirty yellow blanket from a tall kid named Younger Bear, who accepted my trousers and straightway amputated them for use as unjoined leggings, throwing aside the waist and seat. Nobody had use for the boots, which just laid there on the ground and were left in the same position when the camp moved away. If an Indian isn't interested in an item he does not so much as see it, will stumble over it repeatedly without ever considering he might kick it aside.

We never did get breakfast that first morning, for the simple reason that there wasn't any food to be had. The antelope had been ate up totally the night before, and they couldn't afford to do in no more dogs for a spell, seeing as how the ponies was fast disappearing and a certain number of pack animals was required when camp moved. Also Caroline had not returned – for I still thought she might be back at that point; though never once did I entertain the idea she might be killed – and I had nobody to jaw with in my own language.

But before the sun had got far through the sky, I had learned quite a vocabulary of the sign lingo and conversed with Little Horse on such things as could be expressed with the hands. For example, you want to say 'man', so you put up the index finger, with the palm facing inside. Of course I was considerably assisted in learning the lingo by Little Horse's habit of making the sign, then pointing to the thing itself. The motion for 'white man', a finger wiped across the forehead to suggest the brim of a hat, was somewhat difficult to savvy owing to Little Horse himself wearing the felt hat that I had discarded. He kept running his finger along the brim and pointing at me, and I first thought he meant 'your hat', or 'you', before I got it straight. The sign for plain 'man' naturally meant 'Indian man'.

For 'Cheyenne' you run the right index finger across the left as though striping it, for the distinctive arrow-guides used by all

Cheyenne was made of striped feathers from the wild turkey. By the way, in their spoken language Cheyenne don't ever call themselves 'Cheyenne' but rather Tsististas, which means 'the people', or 'the Human Beings'. What anybody else is doesn't concern them.

After our bath, them boys fetched bows and we played war in and out of a buffalo wallow near camp, shooting one another with arrows that didn't have no points. And then we did some wrestling, at which I was none too good and somewhat shy to try too hard, but after getting badly squeezed, I turned to boxing and bloodied at least one brown nose. The latter was the property of Younger Bear, and the event caused him to receive a good deal of jeering, because I'd say Indians are given to that trait even more than whites. I felt sorry for Younger Bear when I saw the ridicule I had let him in for.

Which was a big mistake: I should either never have hit him in the first place or after doing so should have strutted around boasting about it and may be given him some more punishment to consolidate the advantage: that's the Indian way. You should never feel sorry about beating anybody, unless having conquered his body you want his spirit as well. I didn't yet understand that, so throughout the rest of the day I kept trying to shine up to Younger Bear, and the result was I made the first real enemy of my life and he caused me untold trouble for years, for an Indian will make a profession of revenge.

The next thing I remember us boys doing was to go and play camp with a number of little girls. This game is a mimicry of what the grown-ups do. The girls set up miniature tepees and the boys act like husbands, going out on war parties and having mock buffalo hunts in which one boy, playing the animal, carries a prickly pear at the end of a stick. The hunters shoot their arrows at this fruit, and are considered to have brung the buffalo down if they strike the target. Whoever misses, the buffalo lad gets to swat on the hind end with the prickly pear. You can see that whatever the Cheyenne do has a threat of pain in it, if not the realization thereof.

In the earlier doings I had fell in on equal terms, but it wasn't so when it came to play camp, and that I believe was due to Younger Bear, who by common consent was chief of that establishment on account of he could shoot an arrow exceptionally well and he was very convincing when braining a make-believe foe with a nasty-looking war club he had fashioned himself. That's the way a man gets to be a war chief among the Cheyenne: he can fight better than anyone else. He is a chief only in battle. For peace they have another kind of leader. You take Old Lodge Skins, he was a peace chief. The principal war chief of our bunch was Hump. These fellows got along fine, except you'll recall at the whiskey fight as soon as they had a few in their belly, they went for each other. However, when Skin's gun blew up, they forgot about it and went their separate ways.

Anyhow, Younger Bear was at about eleven years of age already very well advanced towards his true profession, and he was a big tall fellow who walked with his chest arched out. I'll say this about the fight I had with him: he could have killed me except that he knew nothing about boxing. But his ignorance wasn't my responsibility; I ain't never been big but I'm shrewd. . . .

It ain't bad being a boy among the Cheyenne. You never get whipped for doing wrong, but rather told: 'That is not the way of the Human Beings.' One time Coyote started to laugh while he was lighting his father's pipe, because a horsefly was crawling on his belly. This was a serious failure of manners on his part, comparable to a white boy's farting loud in church. His Pa laid away the pipe and said: 'On account of your lack of self-control I can't smoke all day without disgusting certain Persons in the other world. I wonder if you aren't a Pawnee instead of a Human Being.' Coyote went out upon the Prairie and stayed there alone all night to hide his shame.

You have got to *do things right* when you are a Cheyenne. A baby can't cry just for the hell of it – the tribe might be lying in concealment at the moment and the sound would give away their position to the enemy. Therefore the women hang them cradleboards on bushes some distance from camp until the youngsters inside develop the idea that crying don't do no good, and get the habit of quiet. Girls need to be trained to control their giggle. I seen Shadow That Comes in Sight line his little daughters up before him and tell them funny stories at which they were supposed to restrain laughter.

At first they all flunked, shrieking like birds; then they got so as to only smirk and simper; and finally, after many sessions, they could hold a stony look towards the most hilarious joke. They was free to enjoy but not to make a demonstration. At the proper time they could laugh their guts out, for an Indian loves him humour and Shadow That Comes in Sight was a great wit.

Other than for that special instruction, the Cheyenne didn't run a school. They never read nor wrote their language, so what would be the purpose? If you wanted a point of history, you went and asked an old man who kept it in his mind. Numbers got boring when you run out of fingers, so to report the size of an enemy war party you had spotted would be something like this: 'The Ute is near the Fasting Place Butte. They are as many as the arrows that Sticks Everything Under His Belt shot at the ghost antelope in the time when the cherries was ripe.' This being a famous story, everybody in Old Lodge Skin's crowd would know within one or two the number of Ute referred to – and in a moment of emergency, when a person tends to fear the unknown, they could connect it up with something familiar. . . .

You understand that I can't give no day-to-day account of my upbringing. It must have took a couple of months to learn to ride without being tied on, and longer to get real proficient with the bow and arrow.

Thomas Berger *Little Big Man*

A HORROR STORY

From Sir Roy Harrod

Sir,—While walking in an eminently respectable part of London, I found myself surrounded by hundreds of children emerging from a comprehensive school at 4 p.m. Shortly afterwards I got on to the top of a bus, which was almost empty, where I was joined by about eight of the children.

They appeared to be of the 14 to 16 age group. Most of them smoked cigarettes; they talked in loud voices and almost every noun was prefixed by the adjective b——. It reminded one of an old-fashioned barrack room; but I do not think that British Tommies ever shouted their favoured epithets on bus tops. One of the children said: "I have got b—— brains and I am going to a b—— university." Another said: "I am a b—— citizen." Presumably he had just attended a class in civics.

Two came to blows and hit each other fiercely. The bigger one finally got the other on to the floor of the bus where he continued to hit him and kicked him.

My patience was exhausted. I said, "You cannot do this sort of thing on a bus," and, seizing him firmly by his shirt collar, I pulled him away from his victim. He at once turned on me and, calling me a "filthy f——" and other obscene names, proceeded to hit and kick me. I am afraid that I do not look younger than my age. None of the others said or did anything. I did not retaliate, mainly, I suppose, because I thought I should be ineffective, but also because I did not want to escalate the episode, since, if it came to the police, I should lack reliable witnesses. Luckily the bus soon stopped at a place where the ruffian wanted to get off. When I got off half a minute later, I felt aches and pains in various places.

What is happening to our education? After all, these children must have already been at school for eight years or more.

I suspect that the schools are too big and that the wrong things are taught. Apart from the inevitably small minority who are destined to be deep scholars or scientists, surely the primary object of education is to instil into our young "citizens" a sense of decency. And this has to be done, not by the formal content of what is taught, which, now that we are getting away from the traditional subjects, cannot in the nature of things be of high educational value, but by the personal influence of the teachers, often operating through side episodes in an insensible manner, on the minds and hearts of the schoolchildren.

I am, &c.,

ROY HARROD

Christ Church, Oxford July 1.

Miss Pringle

'I am sure you have heard all this part of the Bible before. So I shall ask you some questions about it. After all you are supposed to be a little wiser now than you were a year ago. Mount Horeb. What did Moses see on Mount Horeb?'

'A bush, miss, a burning bush'n the Angel of the Lord spoke out of the bush'n –'

'That will do. Yes. Was there anyone in the bush?'

'Miss! Miss! Miss!'

'Wilmot? Yes. Did Moses ever meet him again?'

'Miss! Miss!'

'Jennifer? Yes. On Mount Sinai. Did he see clearly?'

'Miss!'

'Of course not. Even Moses had to be content with "I am that I am."'

'Miss! Miss!'

'What is it, Mountjoy?'

'Please, miss, 'e knew more'n that!'

'Ah –'

I knew then what a fool I was; I knew that if explaining myself to Father Watts-Watt was impossible it was dangerous with Miss Pringle. How could I say – of course you know too, I am only reminding you or perhaps you were only pretending so that one of us would please you by giving more than a dull agreement – but I was too late.

Miss Pringle spread a delighted beam over the class and invited them to share with her the enjoyment of this captive.

'Mountjoy is going to tell us something we do not know, children.'

There was, as she knew, a little ripple at that. She took the ripple just before it had died away.

'Mountjoy knows the Bible much better than we do, of course. After all, he lives very near the church.'

The pendulum began to swing.

'Silence for Mr Mountjoy, children. He is going to explain the Bible to us.'

I could see how red my nose was getting.

'Well, Mountjoy? Aren't you going to give us – the scholarly results of your researches?'

'It was later on, miss, after 'e'd –'

'He'd, Mountjoy, not 'e'd. I'm sure the rector wants you to improve your accent as quickly as possible. Well?'

'E – He wanted to see, miss, but it would 've been too much for – him.'

'What are you talking about, Mountjoy?'

'Miss, Moses, miss.'

Now the laughter flailed. There were cries of Miss Moses that Miss Pringle allowed to increase just this side of riot.

'It was after, miss.'

'After?'

'It would've been too much. So he was hid in a crack in the rock 'n 'e – he saw 'is backparts it say, miss, an' I was going to ask you –'

'What did you say?'

Now I was conscious of the silence, shocked off short.

'It says 'e saw –'

'When did you read that?'

'It was when you told us to learn the, learn the –'

'That was the New Testament lesson, Mountjoy. Why were you looking at the Old?'

'I'd finished, miss, 'n I thought –'

'So you'd finished? You didn't say so. You didn't think to tell me and ask my permission for this, this –'

The topaz shook and glittered.

'Very well, Mountjoy, so you'd finished your verses. Say them.'

But next to my mind as I stood, blinded and dumb in the desk, was the picture of this event as a journey on the wrong track, a huge misunderstanding.

'It was jus' that I wanted to know, miss, the way you said about the veil and all that –'

Say them!'

The blackness of torment turned red. There were no words on my tongue.

'Say them, Mountjoy. "Blessed are the –"'

Don't you understand? I'm on your side, really. I know that the openings are more important to you than the silly plausibilities of explaining away. I know that the book is full of wonder and importance. I am not like Johnny on my left who will take it as read, or Philip in front who is looking at you and wondering how he can learn to use you. My delight is your delight.

Miss Pringle shifted her hand forward to another manual. Here was *vox humana*. We heard this voice sometimes, her wounded voice, voice of Rachel weeping for her children, always the prelude to savagery.

'– thought I could trust you. And so I can, most of you. But there is one boy who cannot be trusted. He uses a lesson – not even an ordinary lesson –'

'But miss! Please, miss –'

Miss Pringle had me standing up where she wanted me. If I did not understand the enormity of my offence, if I was still acquainted with innocence and held the belief that there was room for me somewhere in the scheme of things, nevertheless Miss Pringle felt herself able to undermine me and dedicated herself to that end.

'Come out here in front of the class.'

There was a strange obedience about my two hands that grasped the sides of the seat and helped to lift me. My feet trod obediently and deeper into the dark. She had implied so much in one sentence. By an inflection, a quiver of the topaz she had lifted this episode now above laughing so that the rest of the class had to readjust to seriousness. Miss Pringle had enough showmanship to know that she must not run away from her audience. She gave them time to settle into the new mood by looking so long and searchingly into my face that my blush burned and their silence began to fill with excitement.

'That's what you think the Bible is for then. Oh, no, Mountjoy, don't start to deny it. Do you suppose that I really don't know what you're like? We all know where you come from, Mountjoy, and we were willing to regard it as your misfortune.'

I saw her brown leather shoes that were polished like chestnuts take a little step back.

'But you have brought the place with you. Money has been spent on you, Mountjoy. You have been given a great opportunity. But instead of profiting by it, instead of being grateful, you use your time here, searching through the Bible with a snigger, searching for – for –'

She paused and the silence was deeper still. They all knew what little boys searched the Bible for, because most of them did it. Perhaps that was why my crime – but what was it, I thought? – my crime seemed monstrous to them, too. I thought then, that the trouble was my lack of ability to explain myself. I had a hazy feeling that if only I could find the right words, Miss Pringle would understand and the whole business be disposed of. But I know now that she would not have accepted even the most elaborately accurate explanation. She would have dodged it with furious agility and put me back in the wrong. She was clever and perceptive and compelled and cruel.

'Look at me, I said, "Look at me!"'

'Miss.'

'And then – ! To have the insolence – there is no other word for it – to have the insolence to throw your nastiness in my face!'

She had both white hands up and away. They were cleaning their own fingers as if they would never be clean. The cascade of lace was moving quickly in and out. Now the class understood that this was to be execution in form, public and long drawn out.

Miss Pringle proceeded to the next step. Justice must not only be done, it must be seen to be done. She required evidence of misdoing more than my unfortunate slip in theology. Of course there was one sure way of getting that. Most of the masters and mistresses in that school did not care enough about us to be cruel. They even recognized our right to separate existence and this recognition took a pleasant shape. We were made to keep our exercise books very clean and neat; but we had rough-work books too; and by custom, unspoken, undefined, these books were private. So long as you did not defile them too openly or be outrageously wasteful, they were as private to us as their study to the scholar.

Had she convinced herself? Did she believe by now that I regularly searched the Bible for smut? Did she not understand that we were two of a kind, the earnest metaphysical boy and the tormented spinster, or did she know that and get an added kick from hatred of her own image? Did she really think she would find smut in my rough book; or was she willing to take anything legally wrong if she could find it?

'Get your rough-work book.'

I went back to my desk underground. The silence vibrated and Johnny would not meet my eye. One of my stockings was down round my right ankle. There was no cover on the rough-work book. The first four pages were crumpled and then the pages got flatter and cleaner. Since the first page now did duty for the cover most of my drawing there had worn away.

'Ugh!'

Miss Pringle refused my offer.

'I am not going to touch it, Mountjoy. Put it on the desk. Now. Turn over the pages. Well? What do you say?'

'Miss.'

I began to turn the pages and the class watched eagerly.

Arithmetic and a horse pulling the roller over the town cricket pitch. Some wrongly spelt French verbs, repeated. A cart on the weighing machine outside the Town Hall. Lines. I must not pass notes in class. I must not – the old D H coming round a tower of clouds. Answers to grammar questions. Arithmetic. Latin. Some profiles. A landscape, not drawn, so much as noted down and then elaborated in my own private notation. For how could a pencil convey the peculiar attraction of a white chalk road seen from miles away as it wound up the side of the downs? In the middle distance was a complication of trees and hillocks into which the eye was drawn and into which the troubled spectator could vanish. This was not sketched but put down meticulously. This was so much my own private property that I turned a page hurriedly.

'Wait! Turn back.'

Miss Pringle looked from me to the landscape, then back again.

'Why do you hurry over that page, Mountjoy? Is there something there that you do not wish me to see?'

Silence.

Miss Pringle examined my landscape inch by inch. I could feel the excitement of my fellows, now transformed to bloodhounds on the trail and hot on the back of my neck.

Miss Pringle extended a white finger and began to give the edge of the rough-work book little taps so that it moved round and presented my hillocks, my scalloped downs and deep woodlands to her, upright. Her hand clenched and whipped away. She drew a shuddering breath. She spoke and her voice was deep with awe and passionate anger, with outrage and condemnation.

'Now I see!'

She turned to the class.

'I had a little garden, children, full of lovely flowers. I was glad to work in my little garden because the flowers were so gay and lovely. But I did not know that there were weeds and slugs and snails and hideous slimy crawling things –'

Then she turned on me and tore a vivid gash through my soul with the raw edge of a suddenly savage voice.

'I shall see the rector knows about this, Mountjoy, and I'm going to take you to the headmaster now!'

I waited outside the door with my book while she went into the headmaster's study. I heard their voices and the interview was short. She came out and swept past me and the headmaster told me, sternly, to come in.

'Give me the book.'

He was angry, there was no doubt about that. I suppose she had pointed out what was unnecessary – that we were a mixed school and this sort of thing must be stamped on immediately. I think perhaps he was resigned to having an expulsion on his hands.

He thumbed through the whole book, paused and then thumbed through it again. When he spoke next the gruffness had gone from his voice – or rather was modified as though he knew that he must retain some outrage for the sake of appearances.

'Well, Mountjoy. Which pages does Miss Pringle object to?'

She seemed to object to all of them. I was confused by events and unable to answer.

He thumbed through again. His voice became testy.

'Now listen, Mountjoy. Which page is it? Did you tear it out while you were waiting outside?'

I shook my head. He examined the sewn centre of the book, saw that there was no odd page. He looked back at me.

'Well?'

I found my voice.

'It was that one, sir, there.'

The headmaster bent over the book. He examined my landscape. I saw that the complex centre trapped his sight, too. His eye went forward, plunged through the paper among hillocks and trees. He withdrew from it and his forehead was puzzled. He glanced down at me, then back at the paper. Suddenly he did what Miss Pringle had done – turned the book so that my lovely curved downs were upright, the patch of intricate woodland projecting from them.

We entered a place then which I should now call chaos. I did not know what was the matter, I felt nothing but pain and astonishment. But he, the adult, the headmaster, he did not know anything either. He had taken a pace forward and the ground had disappeared. He had realized something in a flash and the knowledge had presented him at once with a number of insoluble problems. But he was a wise man and did what is always best in such circumstances; that is, nothing. He allowed me to watch his face on which so much became visible. I saw the results of his knowledge even though I could not share it. I saw an appalled realization, I saw impotence to cope, I saw even the beginning of wild laughter.

Then he went and looked out of the window for a little.

'You know, Mountjoy, we don't give you a rough-work book to draw in, do we?'

'Sir.'

'Miss Pringle objects to your wasting so much time with a pencil.'

There was nothing to be said to this. I waited.

'These pages –'

He turned round then and opened the book to show me, but caught sight of something. It was a page where I had drawn as many of the form as I could. Some of them had defeated me; but for one or two I had drawn face after face, elaborating then simplifying so that the final result gave me a deep satisfaction as I sent the passionate message down the pencil. He pushed his spectacles up on his forehead and held the page close.

'That's young Spragg!'

At that the chaos came out of my eyes. It was wet and warm and I could not stop.

'Oh, now, look here!'

I felt round me for a handkerchief but, of course, I had none. I took out my bright school cap and used it instead. When I could see again the headmaster was stroking his moustache and looking defeated. He gave himself another breather out of the window. Gradually I dried up.

'Well there you are then. Keep your drawing within bounds. I think perhaps I'd better keep this rough-work book. And try to –'

He paused for a long time.

'Try to understand that Miss Pringle cares deeply about you all. See if you can please her. Well?'

'Sir.'

'And tell Miss Pringle that I – should be glad to have a word with her in break. Right!'

'Sir.'

'You'd better go and – no. Go now. Straight back to the class as you are. I'll see that you get a new rough-work book.'

I went back to the class with my stained face and gave her the headmaster's message. She ignored me save for one imperious sweep of the hand and a pointing finger. I saw why. In my absence she had my desk moved out of the body of the class. It rested now against the wall right out in front where I should not contaminate the others by my presence. I sank into the seat and was alone. Here I was, with the waves of public disapprobation beating on the back of my neck. I have never minded them since. There I remained for the rest of that term. Sitting alone, I was introduced to the Stuarts. Sitting alone I followed Miss Pringle forward from Gethsemane.

Nowadays I can understand a great deal about Miss Pringle. The male priest at the altar might have taken a comely and pious woman to his bosom; but he chose to withdraw into the fortress of his rectory and have to live with him a slum child, a child whose mother was hardly human. I understand how I must have taxed her, first with my presence, then with my innocence and finally with my talent. But how could she crucify a small boy, tell him that he sat out away from the others because he was not fit to be with them and then tell the story of that other crucifixion with every evidence in her voice of sorrow for human cruelty and wickedness? I can understand how she hated, but not how she kept on such apparent terms of intimacy with heaven.

William Golding *Free Fall*

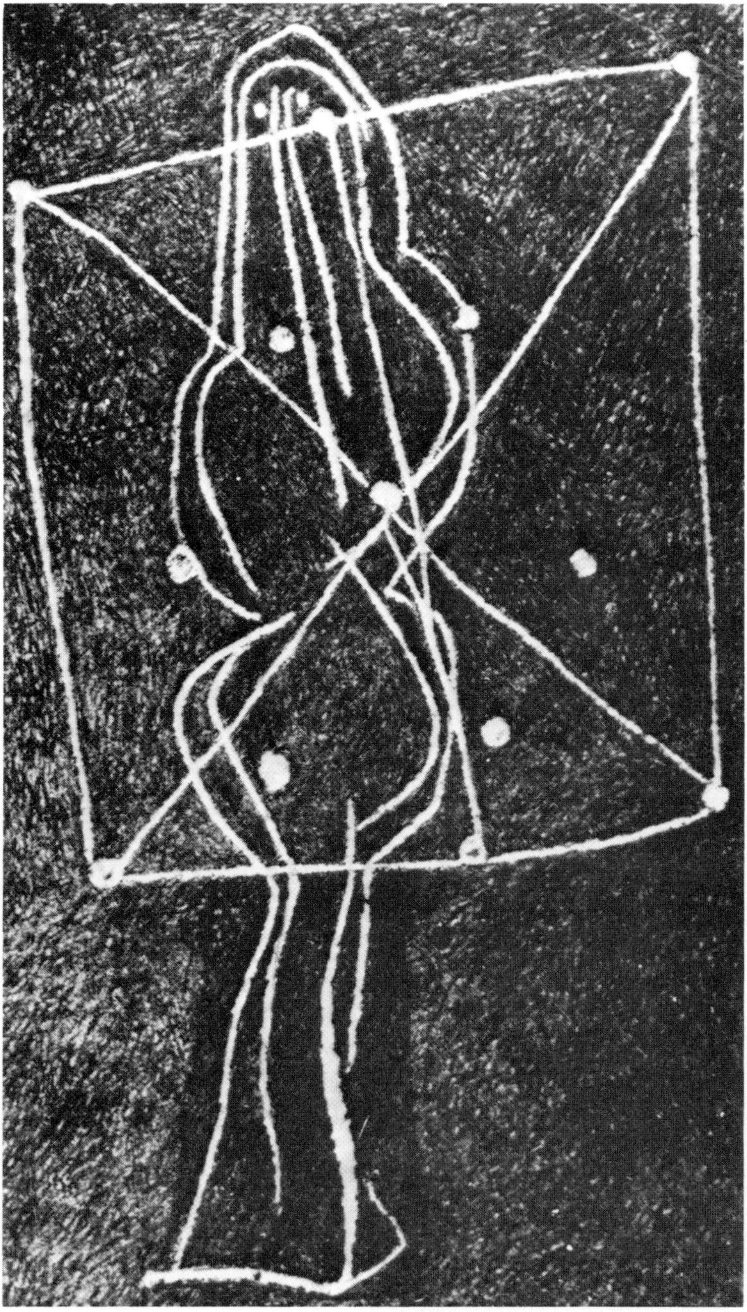

Teaching

My alarm clock rang at seven thirty, but I was up and dressed at seven. It was only a fifteen-minute bus ride from my apartment on 90th Street and Madison Avenue to the school on 119th Street and Madison.

There had been an orientation session the day before. I remember the principal's words. 'In times like these, this is the most exciting place to be, in the midst of ferment and creative activity. Never has teaching offered such opportunities . . . we are together here in a difficult situation. They are not the easiest children, yet the rewards are so great – a smile, loving concern, what an inspiration, felicitous experience.'

I remembered my barren classroom, no books, a battered piano, broken windows and desks, falling plaster and an oppressive darkness.

I was handed a roll book with thirty-six names and thirty-six cumulative record cards, years of judgements already passed on the children, their official personalities. I read through the names, twenty girls and sixteen boys, the 6–1 class, though I was supposed to be teaching the fifth grade and had planned for it all summer. Then I locked the record cards away in the closet. The children would tell me who they were. Each child, each new school year, is potentially many things, only one of which the cumulative record card documents. It is amazing how 'emotional' problems can disappear, how the dullest child can be transformed into the keenest and the brightest into the most ordinary when the prefabricated judgements of other teachers are forgotten.

The children entered at nine and filled up the seats. They were silent and stared at me. It was a shock to see thirty-six black faces before me. No preparation helped. It is one thing to be liberal and talk, another to face something and learn that you are afraid.

The children sat quietly, expectant. *Everything must go well; we must like each other.*

Hands went up as I called the roll. Anxious faces, hostile, indifferent, weary of the ritual, confident of its outcome.

The smartest class in the sixth grade, yet no books.

'Write about yourselves, tell me who you are.' (I hadn't said who I was, too nervous.)

Slowly they set to work, the first directions followed – and if they had refused?

Then arithmetic, the children working silently, a sullen, impenetrable front. *To talk to them, to open up this first day.*

'What would you like to learn this year? My name is Mr Kohl.'

Silence, the children looked up at me with expressionless faces, thirty-six of them crowded at thirty-five broken desks. *This is the smartest class?*

Explain: they're old enough to choose, enough time to learn what they'd like as well as what they have to.

Silence, a restless movement rippled through the class. *Don't they understand? There must be something that interests them, that they care to know more about.*

A hand shot up in a corner of the room.

'I want to learn more about volcanoes. What are volcanoes?

The class seemed interested. I sketched a volcano on the blackboard, made a few comments, and promised to return.

'Anything else? Anyone interested in something?'

Silence, then the same hand.

'Why do volcanoes form?'

And during the answer:

'Why don't we have a volcano here?'

A contest. The class savoured it, I accepted. Question, response, question. I walked towards my inquisitor, studying his mischievous eyes, possessed and possessing smile. I moved to congratulate him, my hand went happily toward his shoulder. I dared because I was afraid.

His hands shot up to protect his dark face, eyes contracted in fear, body coiled ready to bolt for the door and out, down the stairs into the streets.

'But why should I hit you?'

They're afraid too!

Hands relaxed, he looked torn and puzzled. I changed the subject quickly and moved on to social studies – How We Became Modern America.

'Who remembers what America was like in 1800?'

A few children laughed; the rest barely looked at me.

'Can anyone tell me what was going on about 1800? Remember, you studied it last year. Why don't we start more specifically? What do you think you'd see if you walked down Madison Avenue in those days.'

A lovely hand, almost too thin to be seen, tentatively rose.

'Cars?'

'Do you think there were cars in 1800? Remember that was over a hundred and fifty years ago. Think of what you learned last year and try again. Do you think there were cars then?'

'Yes... no... I don't know.'

She withdrew, and the class became restless as my anger rose.

At last another hand.

'Grass and trees?'

The class broke up as I tried to contain my frustration.

'I don't know what you're laughing about – it's the right answer. In those days Harlem was farmland with fields and trees and a few houses. There weren't any roads or houses like the ones outside, or street lights or electricity. There probably wasn't even a Madison Avenue.'

The class was outraged. It was inconceivable to them that there was a time their Harlem didn't exist.

'Stop this noise and let's think. Do you believe that Harlem was here a thousand years ago?'

A pause, several uncertain Noes.

'It's possible that the land was green then. Why couldn't Harlem have been a hundred and fifty or two hundred years ago?'

No response. The weight of Harlem and my whiteness and strangeness hung in the air as I droned on, lost in my righteous monologue. The uproar turned into sullen silence. A slow nervous drumming began at several desks; the atmosphere closed as intelligent faces lost their animation. Yet I didn't understand my mistake, the children's rejection of me and my ideas. Nothing worked. I tried to joke, command, play – the children remained joyless until the bell, then quietly left for lunch.

There was an hour to summon energy and prepare for the afternoon, yet it seemed futile. What good are plans, clever new methods and materials, when the children didn't – wouldn't – care or listen? Perhaps the best solution was to prepare for hostility and silence, become the cynical teacher, untaught by his pupils, ungiving himself, yet protected.

At one o'clock, my tentative cynicism assumed, I found myself once again unprepared for the children who returned and noisily and boisterously avoided me. Running, playing, fighting – they were alive as they tore about the room. I was relieved, yet how to establish order? I fell back on teacherly words.

'You've had enough time to run around. Everybody please go to your seats. We have work to begin!'

No response. The boy who had been so scared during the morning was flying across the back of the room pursued by a demonic-looking child wearing black glasses. Girls stood gossiping in little groups, a tall boy fantasized before four admiring listeners, while a few children wandered in and out of the room. I still knew no one's name.

'Sit down, we've got to work. At three o'clock you can talk all you want to.'

One timid girl listened. I prepared to use one of the teacher's most fearsome weapons and last resources. Quickly white paper was on my desk, the blackboard erased, and numbers from 1 to 10 and 11 to 20 appeared neatly in two columns.

'We're now going to have an *important* spelling test. Please, young lady' – I selected one of the gossipers – 'What's your name? Neomia, pass out the paper. When you get your paper fold it in half, put your heading on it, and number carefully from one to ten and eleven to twenty, exactly as you see it on the blackboard.'

Reluctantly the girls responded, then a few boys, until after the fourth, weariest, repetition of the directions the class was seated and ready to begin – I thought.

Rip, a crumpled paper flew onto the floor. Quickly I replaced it; things had to get moving.

Rip, another paper, rip. I got the rhythm and began quickly, silently replacing crumbled papers.

'The first word is *anchor*. The ship dropped an *anchor*. Anchor.'

'A what?'

'Where?'

'Number two is *final*. Final means last, *final*. Number three is *decision*. He couldn't make a *decision* quickly enough.'

'What decision?'

'What was number two?'

'Final.'

I was trapped.

'Then what was number one?'

'Anchor.'

'I missed a word.'

'Number four is *reason*. What is the *reason* for all this noise?'

'Because it's the first day of school.'

'Yeah, this is too hard for the first day.'

'We'll go on without any comments whatever. The next word is –'

'What number is it?'

'– *direction*. What *direction* are we going. *Direction*.'

'What's four?'

The test seemed endless, but it did end at two o'clock. What next? Once more I needed to regain my strength and composure, and it was still the first day.

'Mr Kohl, can we please talk to each other about the summer? We won't play around. Please, it's only the first day.'

'I'll tell you what, you can talk, but on the condition that everyone, I mean *every single person in the room*, keeps quiet for one whole minute.'

Teacher still had to show he was strong. To prove what? The children succeeded in remaining silent on the third attempt; they proved they could listen. Triumphant, I tried more.

'Now let's try for thirty seconds to think of one colour.'

'You said we could talk!'

'My head hurts, I don't want to think anymore.'

'It's not fair!'

It wasn't. A solid mass of resistance coagulated, frustrating my need to command. The children would not be moved.

'You're right, I'm sorry. Take ten minutes to talk and then we'll get back to work.'

'For ten minutes the children talked quietly; there was time to prepare for the last half hour. I looked over my lesson plans: Reading, 9 to 10; Social Studies, 10 to 10.45, etc., etc. How absurd academic time was in the face of the real day. *Where to look?*

'You like it here, Mr Kohl?'

I looked up into a lovely sad face.

'What do you mean?'

'I mean do you like it here, Mr Kohl, what are you teaching us for?'

Herbert Kohl *36 Children*

The Boy in the Slums

A story of Modern Life in 'Uptown' New York, with Comments, passions, and a Few DIRECT Questions.

Foreword

This story is about a boy namely me, who lives in a apartment in and around the slum area. I feel that other people should be interested in what I have to say and just like me, *try* to do something about it, either by literal or diatribe means. This Book is only to be read by men and women boys and girls who feel deeply serious about segregation and feel that this is no joke. Especially when you are younger you have a better opportunity to speak about and be willing to work for these problems of the slums. Let me ask you some personal questions that may have to do with this book ! ! !

1. Do you live in the slums?

2. How do you think you would feel if you did?

3. Would you rather be rich have mades and servants to take care of you while your mother is away to dinners, niteclubs and business trips? Or would you rather be poor and your mother'd be home to *Love* and take care of you?

Before I wrote the last question down I made sure that at least *I* knew the answer I had a decision to make also because my mother asked that same question just a few days ago and take it from me its not easy to answer a question like that But if jist by mere curiosity you would like to know my answer to this question jist open the pages of this Book and read to your hearts content And do me a favour (just as a friend) tell other people about this Book and *maybe* they may be encouraged to read this Book. (Oh by the way all through this book a word will be in italics and if by any chance you want to know what this word means just look it up in the Back of this Book it is called: 'Alvin's Slang Dictionary').

1. A Introduction to My Mother

I am dreaming and crying in my sleep. I am dreaming because I have nothing better to do and crying because I am dreaming About a problem I had in school, you see I promise myself I'll be good and try to learn more; but everytime I come into the classroom (in my dream) my teacher right then and there starts to pick on me Alvin this or Alvin that. So I say to myself 'enought is to much everyday the same old problem' why that's enough even to make a laughing hyena cry, so I can imagine quite clearly why thats a good enough reason to cry. (wouldn't you if you were in my situation?). Just as I was about to cry in my sleep for the second time unexpectly a hand hit me right on my rear end (I knew it was a hand because I had felt this more than once) of course I woke up and immediately knew that it was time for my brother and my sisters and me to get ready to go to school. My youngest sisters name is Turia she is three years next comes Patsy she is eight years old my next sister's name is Linda She is nine years old then comes my Brother who's name is Gregory he is ten years then comes me Alvin I am eleven years then comes my next sister Sharon she is twelve years going thirteen And last But not least my oldest sister who's name is Brenda she is fourteen. I know you're not interested in my private life but I'll fill you in a little way just to have something interesting to say. The first thing I have to do is head straight for the *Bathe* room – P.S. (By the way the word *Bathe* is just a fancy word I picked up from my teacher 'Mr Herbert Ralph Kohl'. You know I'll let you in on a little secret. Mr Kohl is kind of fancy himself. The reason why I'm telling you this is because my teacher told me to express myself to the *fullest extent*. (thats another fancy word I learned from my teacher) – and the first thing I do in the Bathe room is to wash my face and comb my hair, while my mother is ironing my shirt and pants. Oh by the way my mothers name is Mrs Helen Curry (You can call her *ma* or Mrs Helen cause that what I always call her and she doesn't get mad either). The next thing I do is eat my breakfast which consists of two or three jelly sandwiches and a glass of water or if I'm lucky I'll have a bowl of cereal with *can milk*. At this time it should be 8:30 time to go to school. PS 79 here I come I say as I start out of the door to my building. As I walk along to school which is within walking distance from my house I begin to think of things that could but then again couldn't happen. For example: maybe someday I'll be a scientist or a big businessman or maybe even a engineer or then again the President of the United States or maybe even the mayor. As long as it is somebody important. You see! some people are lucky enought to be born important but not me I'll have to work my way up to what I want to be if I'm even lucky enought to get that far up as a metter of fact I'll even be lucky if I get pass the sixth Grade the way things are going now. If you ever get into a situation similar to mine take my advise don't give up, you have to work for your goal, don't worry you'll never be alone in your problems other people just like you are sharing your same problems. P.S. This is my own personal view of the situation.

I feel I'll have to close this chapter now for I am digging into my long buried problems which you probably wouldn't Be interested in anyhow. But do me a favour read on to the next chapter!

Alvin Lewis Curry quoted in *36 Children* by Herbert Kohl

A is for Arvin, the chipmunk in class;

B is for B[redacted] made his cut fast!

C. is for Clyde, the fagit in Jeans..

D is for Davidi kicked out by a Queen.

E is for Edward, who lives in a can.

F is for Franky who [redacted] tried to play Superman.

G is for "Goofy," who goofed up the walls.

H is for Henry, who swallowed the ball.

When the War Was Over

In Cologne there were actually some houses still standing; somewhere I even saw a moving streetcar, some people too, women even: one of them waved to us; from the Neuss-Strasse we turned into the Ring avenues and drove along them, and I was waiting all the time for the tears, but they didn't come; even the insurance buildings on the Avenue were in ruins, and all I could see of the Hohenstaufen Baths was a few pale-blue tiles. I was hoping all the time the truck would turn off somewhere to the right, for we had lived in the Carolingian Ring; but the truck did not turn, it drove down the Rings: Barbarossa Square, Saxon Ring, Salian Ring, and I tried not to look, and I wouldn't have looked if the truck convoy had not got into a traffic jam up front at Clovis Square and we hadn't stopped in front of the house we used to live in, so I did look. The term 'totally destroyed' is misleading; only in rare cases is it possible to destroy a house totally: it has to be hit three or four times and, to make certain, it should then burn down; the house we used to live in was actually, according to official terminology, totally destroyed, but not in the technical sense. That is to say, I could still recognize it; the front door and the doorbells, and I submit that a house where it is still possible to recognize the front door and doorbells has not, in the strict technical sense, been totally destroyed; but of the house we used to live in there was more to be recognized than the doorbells and the front door: two rooms in the basement were almost intact, on the mezzanine, absurdly enough, even three: a fragment of wall was supporting the third room which would probably not have passed a spirit-level test, our apartment on the second floor had only one room intact, but it was gaping open in front, towards the street; above this a high, narrow gable reared up, bare, with empty window sockets; however, the interesting thing was that two men were moving around in our living room as if their feet were on familiar ground; one of the two men took a picture down from the wall, the Terborch print my father had been so fond of, walked to the front, carrying the picture, and showed it to a third man who was standing down below in front of the house, but this third man shook his head like someone who is not interested in an object being auctioned, and the man up above walked back with the Terborch and hung it up again on the wall; he even straightened the picture; I was touched by this mark of neatness – he even stepped back to make sure the picture was really hanging straight, then nodded in a satisfied way. Meanwhile the second man took the other picture off the wall: an engraving of Lochner's painting of the cathedral, but this one also did not appear to please the third man standing down below; finally the first man, the one who had hung the Terborch back on the wall, came to the front, formed a megaphone with his hands and shouted: 'Piano in sight!' and the man below laughed, nodded, likewise formed a megaphone with his hands and shouted: 'I'll get the straps.' I could not see the piano, but I knew where it stood: on the right in the corner I couldn't see into and where the man with the Lochner picture was just disappearing.

'Whereabouts in Cologne do you live?' asked the Belgian guard.

'Oh, somewhere over there,' I said, gesturing vaguely in the direction of the western suburbs.

'Thank God, now we're moving again,' said the guard. He picked up his submachine gun, which he had placed on the floor of the truck, and straightened his cap. The lion of Flanders on the front of his cap was rather dirty. As we turned into Clovis Square I could see why there had been a traffic jam: some kind of raid seemed to be going on. English military police cars were all over the place, and civilians were standing in them with their hands up, surrounded by a sizeable crowd, quiet yet tense: a surprisingly large number of people in such a silent, ruined city.

'That's the black market,' said the Belgian guard. 'Once in a while they come and clean it up.'

Heinrich Boll *When the War Was Over. Translated from the German by Leila Vennewitz*

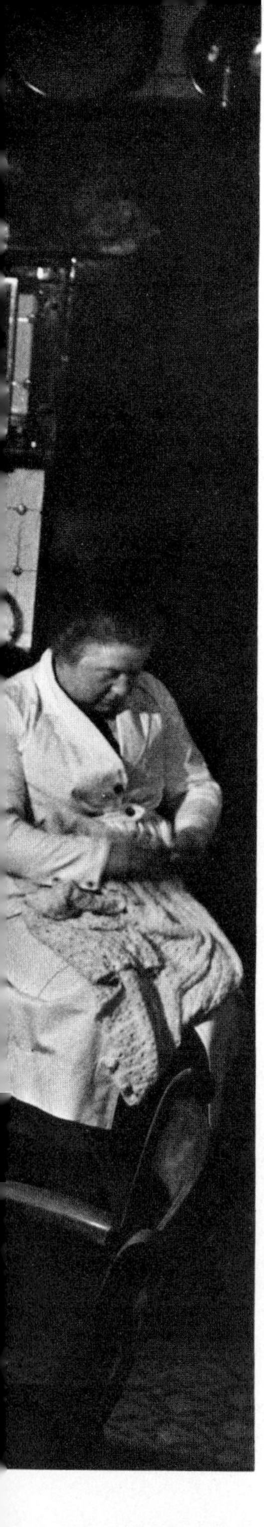

Sent Away to Service

It were nothing for a girl to be sent away to service when she were eleven year old. This meant leaving the family as she had never been parted from for a day in her life before, and going to some place miles away to be treated like something as ha'n't got as much sense or feeling as a dog. I'm got nothing against girls going into good service. In my opinion, good service in a properly run big house were a wonderful training for a lot o' girls who never would ha' seen anything different all the days o' their lives if they ha'n't a-gone. It were better than working on the land, then, and if it still existed now, I reckon I'd rather see any o' my daughters be a good housemaid or a well-trained parlourmaid than a dolled-up shop assistant or a factory worker. But folks are too proud to work for other folks, now, even if it's to their own advantage, though as far as I can see you are still working for other folks, whatever you're a-doing. Such gals as us from the fen din't' get 'good' service though, not till we'd learnt a good deal the hard way. Big houses di'n't want little girls of eleven, even as kitchen maids, so the first few years 'ad to be put in somewhere else, afore you got even that amount o' promotion. Big houses expected good service, but you got good treatment in return. It wern't like that at the sort o' place my friends had to go to. Mostly they went to the farmers's houses within ten or twenty mile from where they'd been born. These farmers were a jumped up, proud lot who di'n't know how to treat the people who worked for 'em. They took advantage o' the poor peoples' need to get their girls off their hands to get little slaves for nearly nothing. The conditions were terrible. One little girl I know'd went when she were eleven to a great lonely farmhouse 'on the highlands', miles from anywhere. The very next day after she got there, the grandmother o' the household died and were laid out on the bed straight away. Then the heartless woman of the house sent poor little Eva to scrub the floor o' the room where the corpse laid. She were frit to death, an' no wonder, but she 'ad to do it. When she were cleaning under the bed, the corpse suddenly rumbled and groaned as the wind passed out of it, and to Eva's dying day she never forgot the terror o' that moment. I can't think there were many folks as 'ould 'ave bin as cruel as that, but when I remember the general conditions o' such poor little mites, it makes me think again.

I 'ad one friend as I were particularly fond of, called for some reason as I never did know, 'Shady'. Shady's adventures at service 'ould fill a book on their own. They lived close to us, and we'd allus bin friends, so she were nearly like my sister. She went to service when she were about thirteen, to a lonely, outlaying fen farm in a place called Black-bushe. The house were a mile or more from the road, and there were no other house near by. A big open farm yard were all around it on three sides, and at the back door, it opened straight into the main drain, about twelve feet wide and ten feet deep with sides like the wall of a house. There were no escape there. Her duties were as follows.

She were woke up at 6 a.m. every morning by the horsekeeper, who had walked several mile to work already, and used a clothes prop to rattle on her window to rouse her. She had to get up straight away and light the scullery fire in the big, awkward old range, that she 'ad to clean and black-lead afore it got too hot. Then she put the kettle on to get tea made for 6.30 a.m. for the horsekeeper, who baited the horses first, come in for his breakfast at 6.30, and went out and yoked his horses so as to be away to work in the fields by seven o'clock. While the kettle boiled, she started to scrub the bare tiles o' the kitchen floor. This were a terrible job. There were no hot water, and the kitchen were so big there seemed nearly an acre of it to scrub – and when you'd finished that, there'd be the dairy, just as big and the scullery as well. Skirts were long and got in the way as you knelt to scrub, and whatever you done you cou'n't help getting wet. In the winter you'd only have the light o' candles to do it by, and the kitchen 'ould be so cold the water 'ould freeze afore you could mop it up properly.

At 6.30 the horsekeeper come in for his tea, and as soon as he'd gone Shady had to start getting breakfast for the family. When they'd had theirs, she could have hers, which was only bread and butter, and the tea left in the pot by the family. If there were little children in the house, she'd be expected to have them with her and give them their breakfast while she had her own. After breakfast she washed up, including all the milk utensils and so on from the dairy, and then started the housework. Very often another woman from the farm 'ould be employed to help with this and to do the washing, while the missus done the cooking and housekeeping duties. On churning days Shady had to get up extra early to make time to fit the churning in. There were no time off at all during the day, and after supper she had to wash up all the things and prepare for next morning. This meant cleaning all the family's boots and shoes, and getting things ready for breakfast next morning. Farmers cured their own bacon and hams, so she would be given the bacon taken from a side 'in-cut', but the custom was to have fried potatoes for breakfast with the bacon. These were supposed to be the 'taters' left over from supper, but there were never enough left, so one of her evening jobs was allus to peel and boil a big saucepan of potatoes to fry next morning. As I'm said afore, she was allowed only bread and butter for her own breakfast.

Then if she had any time before it was bed time, she had to sit by herself in the cold dark kitchen in front of a dying fire that she weren't allowed to make up, except in lambing time. In lambing time it were took for granted that any lambs as were weakly 'ould be looked after in the kitchen, and while the season lasted the old shepherd 'ould come in and set in the kitchen while he waited for his ewes to lamb. I'm 'eard Shady say 'ow she dreaded this. The shepherd were a dirty, nasty, vulgar old man as no decent girl were safe with; but at the best o' times he weren't very pleasant to have to sit with, stinking o' the sheep, belching and blowing off, and every now and then getting up and straddling over to make water in the kitchen sink. The only other choice she 'ad were to go to bed, once she were sure she wou'n't be needed again, but that di'n't offer such pleasant prospects either. Maids' rooms were allus at the very top, at the back on the north side o' the house. There were nothing in them but a bed with a hard old flock mattress, a table by the side of it, and the tin trunk the girl had brought her clothes in. It was icy cold in winter, and Shady weren't the only one o' my friends an' acquaintances by a long way as told me they slept in all their clothes to keep warm an' all.

Though 'the woman' done the washing for the family, she di'n't do Shady's. She weren't allowed to do it herself, but 'ad to send it home to her mother once a week by the carrier. This took most o' Shady's 'afternoon off', because she had to walk up to the high road and meet the carrier's cart, often hanging about an hour or more waiting for him, to get her dirty washing exchanged for clean. Sometimes her mother 'ould walk the five or six mile with the clean washing, just to see her for a few minutes afore walking it all the other way. On the first time she did this, she found Shady on her knees scrubbing the kitchen floor. Shady got up to greet her, and her mother lifted her skirt and said 'Let's 'ev a look at yer britches.' As the poor mother expected, they were wet through with cold water and black as a soot bag with the constant kneeling and scrubbing and blackleading. It was a sort o' test to the experienced mother's eye o' what sort of a 'place' she were forced to leave her daughter in. I don't know which of 'em 'ould suffer most, the mother or the daughter. But there were no help for it, and every girl as left home were one less mouth to feed. If she behaved herself and stuck it out a whole year, there did come a day when she'd draw her year's wages, which stood then at five pound.

Sybil Marshall *Fenland Chronicle*

A Union Man

We used to start work at half past six in the morning; but on a Monday morning we invariably couldn't start until nine o'clock because there was no steam. The reason for this was that, over the weekend, the fires had gone down a bit, and because they were economizing on coal they hadn't started them up early enough. So we was sitting down, messing about, and I said, 'Well, I'm going to stop this anyway.'

Now on a Friday it was the usual custom to take your workbook to the foreman, who was housed in an office which overlooked the whole of the shop. You had to walk up three steps, you see – all part of the set-up to show the importance of the man in charge. And I went up these three steps to his office with everybody watching, because they knew what I was going for. I put my book to him and I said, 'Two hours' lost time.' He said, 'Two hours' lost time? What? What for?' I said, 'The two hours I came on Monday morning and couldn't work.' So he threw the book at me and said, 'Well you're not having that.' And I threw the book back and said, 'I'm not going till I do.' This went on for several minutes. Eventually, with the most

crimson of faces, he said, 'There you are'; and he gave me an hour and a half, and threw the book back in fury. That was the start of getting payment for lost time, although it was many months before anybody got it.

At thirteen, in those days, you took the labour examination to see whether you was fit to leave. And if you hadn't reached a certain standard they made you stay at school until you was fourteen. I left at thirteen and went to work at the factory where my father worked. And I worked there for twenty-nine years.

The work I did when I first started there was to turn stockings – that was the old-fashioned cashmere hose that the women wore and the half-hose which men wore. We turned them from the side which was dyed, which was the wrong side, to the right side. For this we had what was called a peg: it was really a piece of wood that one leant on on the bench. And you did it by putting the finger of your left hand on top of the sock and turning it over. Then you bundled them in five dozens. For which we got sixpence for a hundred dozen pairs – that's 2400 socks. We got pretty adept at this job and on occasions when we were really speedy we'd do fifty dozens in an hour.

When I first went, I got a penny an hour, but after a month or two you went on what we call your own time, piece rate. I worked from six in the morning till quarter to nine at night on this job. We had half an hour for breakfast, an hour for dinner and had a tea while we were working. In the hour we had for dinner I walked home, which was about a mile each way.

Mind you, it hasn't changed that much. We're still fighting a lot of the same old battles. The other day I had a telephone call from a man who said he worked at this firm and there were some of them wanted to join the union. So we arranged a meeting and these chaps came along and told me of circumstances that I didn't believe existed anywhere in the country today – it was almost unbelievable. The manager of this firm is a Pole – it's a big combine – and he just got these men to do everything at his bidding, no questions, no nothing. They'd go to work, say on a Saturday morning, and at ten o'clock he'd say, 'You can finish now, come back at five' – on a Saturday afternoon. And the men invariably did. If anyone protested, within a week they'd finished. If anyone was ill for a fortnight, they didn't want them back – their place would've been filled. Now this is the pith of the story: these men, almost to a man, were ex-miners, ex-militant miners, whose mine had closed. And they said to me, 'This is the position: he's told us now he's got six hundred names for the factory, and another colliery's closing next month (which is now indeed closed) and there'll be another six hundred from there.

Of couse it was a very modern factory and I expect any visitor would say, 'What a delightful place to work in' – but he just treated these people like dogs.

Jack Charlesworth

Hard Travelling

Everybody talks of the Crash of '29. In small towns out West, we didn't know there was a crash. What did the stock market mean to us? Not a dang thing. If you were in Cut Bank, Montana, who owned stock?

I finished high school in 1930, and I walked out into this thing. . . .

It got tougher. We didn't know how to make out in the city. It was terrifying. There were great queues of guys in soup lines. We didn't know how to join a soup line. We – my two brothers and I – didn't see ourselves that way. We had middle-class ideas without a middle-class income.

We ended up in San Francisco in 1931. I tried to get a job on the docks. I was a big husky athlete, but there just wasn't any work. Already by that time, if you were looking for a job at a Standard Oil Service Station, you had to have a college degree. It was that kind of market. . . .

We grab the midnight freight and get off at Phoenix. It's a hostile town, so we beat it.

refrigerator wagon

We make an orange freight. We rode in the reefer. Clear to Kansas City. It goes like a bat out of hell, a rough ride. We broke through the wire netting and ate the oranges. We got vitamins like mad. But your mouth gets burnt by that acid juice and our teeth get so damn sore from that ride. By the time we got off at K.C., I could hardly close my mouth.

We catch a train into Kansas City, Kansas, that night. At the stops, coloured people were gettin' on the trains and throwin' off coal. You could see people gatherin' the coal. You could see the railroad dicks were gettin' tough.

Hal and I are ridin' on the top of a boxcar. It's a fairly nice night. All of a sudden there's a railroad dick with a flashlight that reaches a thousand miles. Bam! Bam! He starts shooting. We hear the bullets hitting the cars, bam! like that. I throw my hands up and start walking towards that light. Hal's behind me. The guy says, 'Get off.' I said, 'Christ, I can't.' This thing's rollin' fifty miles an hour or more. He says, 'Jump.' I says, 'I can't.' He says, 'Turn around and march ahead.' He marches us over the top. There's a gondola, about eight feet down. He says, 'Jump.' So I jumped and I landed in wet sand, up to my knees.

We come to a little town in Nebraska, Beatrice. It's morning. I'm chilled to the bone. We crawl into a railroad sandbox, almost frozen to death. We dry out, get warmed up, and make the train again. We pull into Omaha. It's night. All of a sudden, the train is surrounded by deputies, with pistols. The guy says, 'Get in those trucks.' I said, 'What for? We haven't done anything.' He said, 'You're not going to jail. You're going to the Transient Camp.'

Hell yes. Everybody was a criminal. You stole, you cheated through. You were getting by, survival. Stole clothes off lines, stole milk off back porches, you stole bread. I remember going through Tucumcari, New Mexico, on a freight. We made a brief stop. There was a grocery store, a supermarket kind of thing for those days. I beat it off the train and came back with rolls and crackers. The guy is standing in the window shaking his fist at you.

It wasn't a big thing, but it created a coyote mentality. You were a predator. You had to be. The coyote is crafty. He can be fantastically courageous and a coward at the same time. He'll run, but when he's cornered, he'll fight. I grew up where they were hated, 'cause they'd kill sheep. They'll kill a calf, get in the chicken pen. They're mean. But how else does a coyote stay alive? He's not as powerful as a wolf. He has a small body. He's in such bad condition, a dog can run him down. He's not like a fox. A coyote is nature's victim as well as man's. We were coyotes in the Thirties, the jobless.

Ed Paulsen

When I was hoboing, I would lay on the side of the tracks and wait until I could see the train comin'. I would always carry a bottle of water in my pocket and a piece of tape or rag to keep it from bustin' and put a piece of bread in my pocket, so I wouldn't starve on the way. I would ride all day and all night long in the hot sun.

I'd ride atop a boxcar and went to Los Angeles, four days and four nights. The Santa Fe, we'd go all the way with Santa Fe. I was goin' over the hump and I was so hungry and weak 'cause I was goin' into the d.t.'s, and I could see snakes draggin' through the smoke. I was sayin', 'Lord, help me, Oh Lord, help me,' until a white hobo named Callahan, he was a great big guy, looked like Jack Dempsey, and he got a scissors on me, took his legs and wrapped 'em around me. Otherwise, I was about to fall off the Flyer into a cornfield there. I was sick as a dog until I got into Long Beach, California.

Black and white, it didn't make any difference who you were, 'cause everybody was poor. All friendly, sleep in a jungle. We used to take a big pot and cook food, cabbage, meat and beans all together. We all set together, we made a tent. Twenty-five or thirty would be out on the side of the rail, white and coloured. They didn't have no mothers or sisters, they didn't have no home, they were dirty, they had overalls on, they didn't have no food, they didn't have anything.

Sometimes we sent one hobo to walk, to see if there were any jobs open. He'd come back and say: Detroit, no jobs. He'd say: they're hirin' in New York City. So we went to New York City. Sometimes ten or fifteen of us would be on the train. And I'd hear one of 'em holler. He'd fall off, he'd get killed. He was trying to get off the train, he thought he was gettin' home there. He heard a sound. (Imitates train whistle, a long, low, mournful sound.)

And then I saw a railroad police, a white police. They call him Texas Slim. He shoots you off all trains. We come out of Lima, Ohio. . . . Lima Slim, he would kill you if he catch you on any train. Sheep train or any kind of merchandise train. He would shoot you off, he wouldn't ask you to get off.

I was in chain gangs and been in jail all over the country. I was in a chain gang in Georgia. I had to pick cotton for four months, for just hoboin' on a train. Just for vag. They gave me thirty-five cents and a pair of overalls when I got out. Just took me off the train, the guard. 1930, during the Depression, in the summertime. Yes, sir, thirty-five cents, that's what they gave me.

I knocked on people's doors. They'd say, 'What do you want? I'll call the police.' And they'd put you in jail for vag. They'd make you milk cows, thirty or ninety days. Up in Wisconsin, they'd do the same thing. Alabama, they'd do the same thing. California, anywhere you'd go. Always in jail, and I never did nothin'.

A man had to be on the road. Had to leave his wife, had to leave his mother, leave his family just to try to get money to live on. But he'd

230

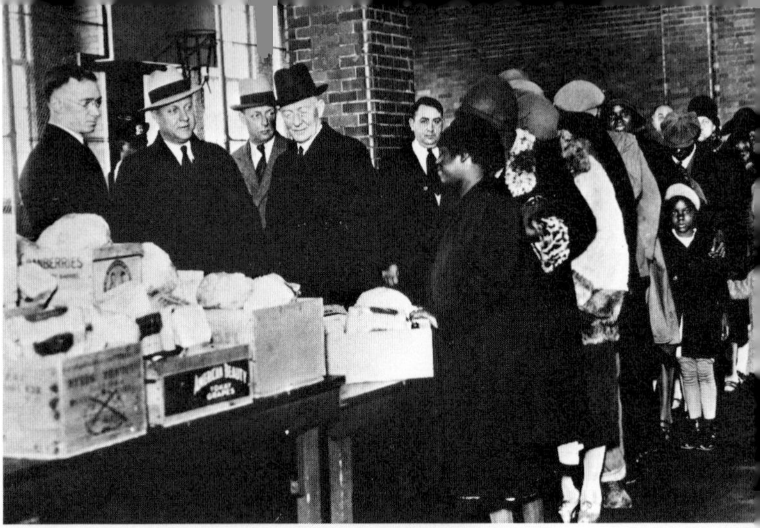

HOME
UNEMPLOYED
BUY
APPLES

think: my dear mother, tryin' to send her money, worryin' how she's starvin'.

The shame I was feeling. I walked out because I didn't have a job. I said, 'I'm goin' out in the world and get me a job.' And God help me, I couldn't get anything. I wouldn't let them see me dirty and ragged and I hadn't shaved. I wouldn't send 'em no picture.

I'd write: 'Dear Mother, I'm doin' wonderful and wish you're all fine.' That was in Los Angeles and I was sleeping under some steps and there was paper over me. This is the slum part, Negroes live down there. And my ma, she'd say, 'Oh, my son is in Los Angeles, he's doin' pretty fair.'

And I was with a bunch of hoboes, drinkin' canned heat. I wouldn't eat two or three days, 'cause I was too sick to eat. It's a wonder I didn't die. But I believe in God.

I went to the Hospital there in Los Angeles. They said, 'Where do you live?' I'd say, 'Travellers Aid, please send me home.' Police says, 'OK, put him in jail.' I'd get ninety days for vag. When I was hoboing I was in jail two-thirds of the time. Instead of sayin' five or ten days, they'd say sixty or ninety days. 'Cause that's free labour. Pick the fruit or pick the cotton, then they'd turn you loose.

'Cause I picked cotton down in Arkansas when I was a little bitty boy and I saw my dad, he was workin' all day long. Two dollars is what one day the poor man would make. A piece of salt pork and a barrel of flour for us and that was McGehee, Arkansas.

God knows, when he'd get that sack he'd pick up maybe two, maybe three hundred pounds of cotton a day, gettin' snake bit and everything in that hot sun. And all he had was a little house and a tub to keep the water. 'Cause I went down there to see him in 1930. I got tired of hoboing and went down to see him and my daddy was all grey and didn't have no bank account and no Blue Cross. He didn't have nothin', and he worked himself to death.

It seems like yesterday to me, but it was 1930.

Louis Banks quoted in *Hard Times: An Oral History of the Great Depression*, by Studs Terkel

A History Lesson

Kings
like golden gleams
made with a mirror on the wall.

A non-alcoholic pope,
knights without arms,
arms without knights.

The dead like so many strained noodles,
a pound of those fallen in battle,
two ounces of those who were executed,

several heads
like so many potatoes
shaken into a cap –

Geniuses conceived
by the mating of dates
are soaked up by the ceiling into infinity

to the sound of tinny thunder,
the rumble of bellies,
shouts of hurrah,

empires rise and fall
at a wave of the pointer,
the blood is blotted out –

And only one small boy,
who was not paying the least attention,
will ask
between two victorious wars:

And did it hurt in those days too?

Miroslav Holub *Translated from the Czech by George Theiner*

THE BATTLE OF MEEANEE.

Slightly Unstuck in Time

Billy Pilgrim padded downstairs on his blue and ivory feet. He went into the kitchen, where the moonlight called his attention to a half bottle of champagne on the kitchen table, all that was left from the reception in the tent. Somebody had stoppered it again. 'Drink me,' it seemed to say.

So Billy uncorked it with his thumbs. It didn't make a pop. The champagne was dead. So it goes.

Billy looked at the clock on the gas stove. He had an hour to kill before the saucer came. He went into the living room, swinging the bottle like a dinner bell, turned on the television. He came slightly

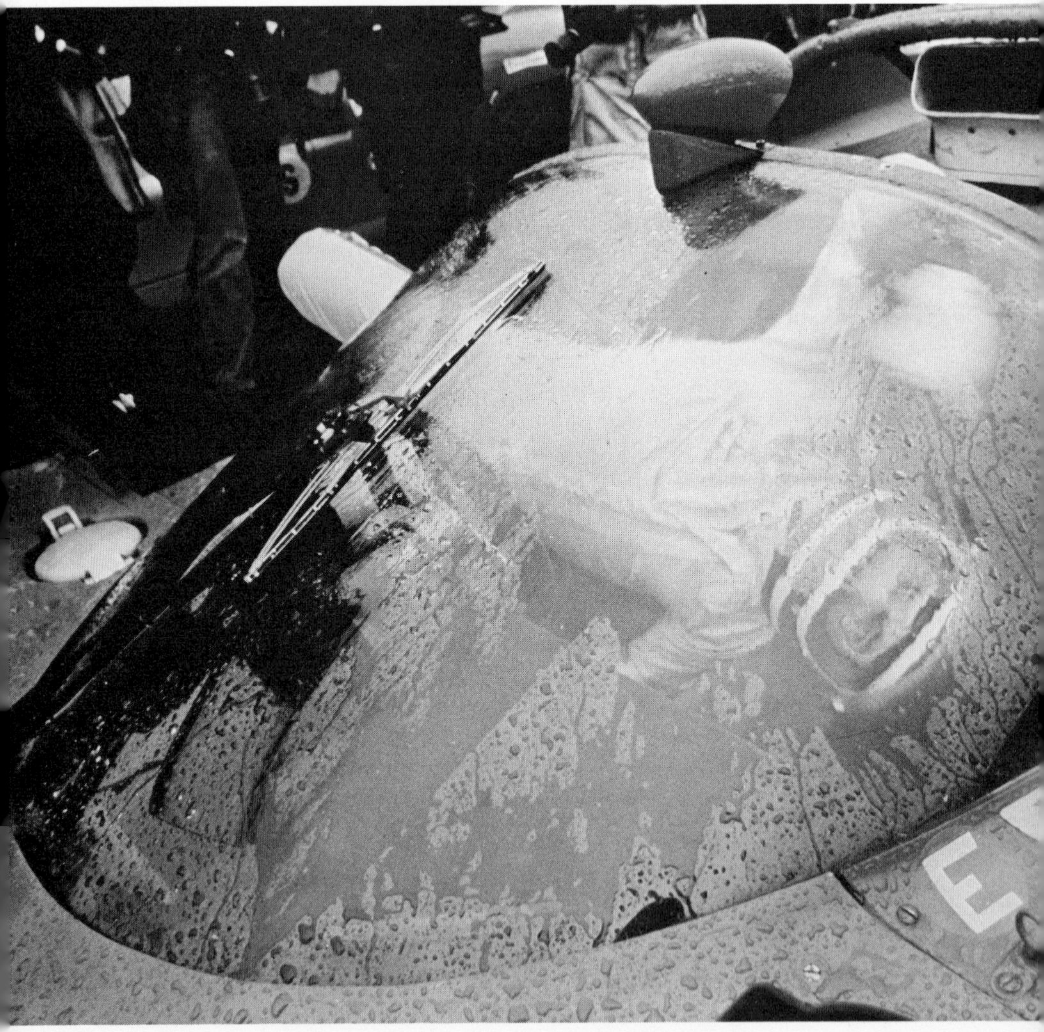

unstuck in time, saw the late movie backwards, then forwards again. It was a movie about American bombers in the Second World War and the gallant men who flew them. Seen backwards by Billy, the story went like this:

American planes, full of holes and wounded men and corpses took off backwards from an airfield in England. Over France, a few German fighter planes flew at them backwards, sucked bullets and shell fragments from some of the planes and crewmen. They did the same for wrecked American planes on the ground, and those planes flew up backwards to join the formation.

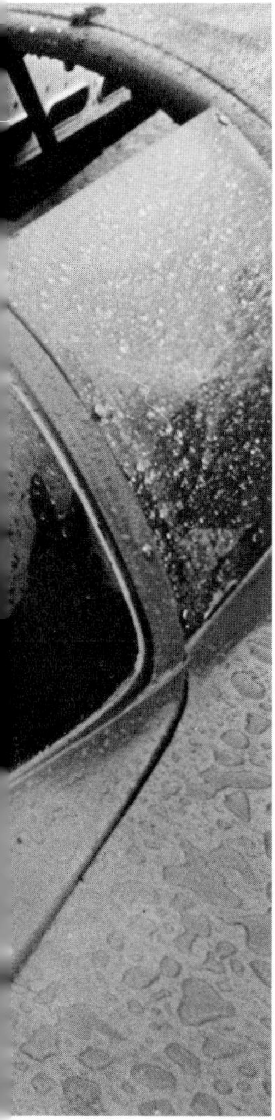

The formation flew backwards over a German city that was in flames. The bombers opened their bomb bay doors, exerted a miraculous magnetism which shrunk the fires, gathered them into cylindrical steel containers, and lifted the containers into the bellies of the planes. The containers were stored neatly in racks. The Germans below had miraculous devices of their own, which were long steel tubes. They used them to suck more fragments from the crewmen and the planes. But there were still a few wounded Americans, though, and some of the bombers were in bad repair. Over France, though, German fighters came up again, made everything and everybody as good as new.

When the bombers got back to their base, the steel cylinders were taken from the racks and shipped back to the United States of America, where factories were operating night and day, dismantling the cylinders, separating the dangerous contents into minerals. Touchingly, it was mainly women who did this work. The minerals were then shipped to specialists in remote areas. It was their business to put them into the ground, to hide them cleverly, so they would never hurt anybody ever again.

The American fliers turned in their uniforms, became high-school kids. And Hitler turned into a baby, Billy Pilgrim supposed. That wasn't in the movie. Billy was extrapolating. Everybody turned into a baby, and all humanity, without exception, conspired biologically to produce two perfect people named Adam and Eve, he supposed.

Billy saw the war movies backwards then forwards – and then it was time to go out into his backyard to meet the flying saucer. Out he went, his blue and ivory feet crushing the wet salad of the lawn. He stopped, took a swig of the dead champagne. It was like 7-Up. He would not raise his eyes to the sky, though he knew there was a flying saucer from Tralfamadore up there. He would see it soon enough, inside and out, and he would see, too, where it had come from soon enough – soon enough.

Overhead he heard the cry of what might have been a melodious owl, but it wasn't a melodious owl. It was a flying saucer from Tralfamadore, navigating in both space and time, therefore seeming to Billy Pilgrim to have come from nowhere all at once. Somewhere a big dog barked.

The saucer was one hundred feet in diameter, with portholes around its rim. The light from the portholes was a pulsing purple. The only noise it made was the owl song. It came down to hover over Billy, and to enclose him in a cylinder of pulsing purple light. Now there was the sound of a seeming kiss as an airtight hatch in the bottom of the saucer was opened. Down snaked a ladder that was outlined in pretty lights like a Ferris wheel.

Billy's will was paralysed by a zap gun aimed at him from one of the portholes. It became imperative that he take hold of the bottom rung of the sinuous ladder, which he did. The rung was electrified, so that Billy's hands locked on to it hard. He was hauled into the airlock, and machinery closed the bottom door. Only then did the ladder, wound on to a reel in the airlock, let him go. Only then did Billy's brain start working again.

There were two peepholes inside the airlock – with yellow eyes pressed to them. There was a speaker on the wall. The Tralfamadorians had no voice boxes. They communicated telepathically. They were able to talk to Billy by means of a computer and a sort of electric organ which made every Earthling speech sound.

'Welcome aboard, Mr Pilgrim,' said the loudspeaker. 'Any questions?'

Billy licked his lips, thought a while, inquired at last: 'Why me?'

'That is a very *Earthling* question to ask, Mr Pilgrim. Why *you*? Why *us* for that matter? Why *anything*? Because this moment simply *is*. Have you ever seen bugs trapped in amber?'

'Yes.' Billy, in fact, had a paperweight in his office which was a blob of polished amber with three ladybugs embedded in it.

'Well, here we are, Mr Pilgrim, trapped in the amber of this moment. There is no *why*.'

They introduced an anesthetic into Billy's atmosphere now, to put him to sleep. They carried him to a cabin where he was strapped to a yellow Barca-Lounger which they had stolen from a Sears and Roebuck warehouse. The hold of the saucer was crammed with other stolen merchandise, which would be used to furnish Billy's artificial habitat in a zoo on Tralfamadore.

The terrific acceleration of the saucer as it left Earth twisted Billy's slumbering body, distorted his face, dislodged him in time, sent him back to the war.

When he regained consciousness, he wasn't on the flying saucer. He was in a boxcar crossing Germany again.

Some people were rising from the floor of the car, and others were lying down. Billy planned to lie down, too. It would be lovely to sleep. It was black in the car, and black outside the car, which seemed to be going about two miles an hour. The car never seemed to go any faster than that. It was a long time between clicks, between joints in the track. There would be a click, and then a year would go by, and then there would be another click.

The train often stopped to let really important trains bawl and hurtle by. Another thing it did was stop on sidings near prisons, leaving a few cars there. It was creeping across all of Germany, growing shorter all the time.

Billy let himself down oh so gradually now, hanging onto the diagonal cross-brace in the corner in order to make himself seem nearly weightless to those he was joining on the floor. He knew it was important that he make himself nearly ghostlike when lying down. He had forgotten why, but a reminder soon came.

'Pilgrim –,' said a person he was about to nestle with, 'is that *you* ?'

Billy didn't say anything, but nestled very politely, closed his eyes.

'God damn it,' said the person. 'That *is* you isn't it ?' He sat up and explored Billy rudely with his hands. 'It's you all right. Get the hell out of here.'

Now Billy sat up, too – wretched, close to tears.

'Get out of here ! I want some sleep !'

'Shut up,' said somebody else.

'I'll shut up when Pilgrim gets away from here.'

So Billy stood up again, clung to the cross-brace. 'Where *can* I sleep ?' he asked quietly.

'Not with me.'

'Not with me, you son of a bitch,' said somebody else. 'You yell. You kick.'

'I do ?'

'You're goddam right you do. And whimper.'

'I do ?'

'Keep the hell away from here, Pilgrim.'

And now there was an acrimonious madrigal, with parts sung in all quarters of the car. Nearly everybody, seemingly, had an atrocity story of something Billy Pilgrim had done to him in his sleep. Everybody told Billy Pilgrim to keep the hell away.

So Billy Pilgrim had to sleep standing up, or not sleep at all. And food had stopped coming in through the ventilators, and the days and nights were colder all the time.

Kurt Vonnegut *Slaughterhouse-Five*

The Time Merry-Go-Round

They hit the carnival grounds at a good twenty miles an hour, give or take a mile, the nephew in the lead, Jim close behind and Will further back. Gasping, shotgun blasts of fatigue in his feet, his head, his heart.

The nephew, running scared, looked back, not smiling.

Fooled him, thought Will, he figured I wouldn't follow, figured I'd call the police, get stuck, not be believed or run hide. Now he's scared I'll beat the tar out of him, and wants to jump on that ride and run around getting older and bigger than me. Oh, Jim, Jim, we got to stop him, keep him young, tear his skin off!

But he knew from Jim's running there'd be no help from Jim. Jim wasn't running after nephews. He was running towards free rides.

The nephew vanished around a tent far ahead. Jim followed. By the time Will reached the midway, the merry-go-round was popping to life. In the pulse, the din, the squeal-around of music the small fresh-faced nephew rode the great platform in a swirl of midnight dust.

Jim, ten feet back, watched the horses leap, his eyes striking fire from the high-jumped stallion's eyes.

The merry-go-round was going *forward* !

Jim *leaned* at it.

'Jim,' cried Will.

The nephew swept from sight borne around by the machine. Drifted back again he stretched out pink fingers urging softly : '. . . Jim . . . ?'

Jim twitched one foot forward.

'No !' Will plunged.

He knocked, seized, held Jim ; they toppled ; they fell in a heap.

The nephew, surprised, whisked on in darkness, one year older. One year older, thought Will, on the earth, one year taller, bigger, meaner !

'Oh God, Jim, quick !' He jumped up, ran to the control box, the complex mysteries of brass switch and porcelain covering and sizzling wires. He struck the switch. But Jim, behind, babbling, tore at Will's hands. 'Will, you'll spoil it ! No !'

Jim knocked the switch full back.

Will spun and slapped his face. Each clenched each other's elbows, rocked, failed. They fell against the control box.

Will saw the evil boy, a year older still, glide around into the night. Five or six more times round and he'd be bigger than the two of them !

'Jim, he'll kill us !'

'Not me, no!'

Will felt a sting of electricity. He yelled, pulled back, hit the switch handle. The control box spat. Lightning jumped to the sky. Jim and Will, flung by the blast, lay watching the merry-go-round run wild.

The evil boy whistled by, clenched to a brass tree. He cursed. He spat. He wrestled with wind, with centrifuge. He was trying to clutch his way through the horses, the poles, to the outer rim of the carousel. His face came, went, came, went. He clawed. He brayed. The control box erupted blue showers. The carousel jumped and bucked. The nephew slipped. He fell. A black stallion's steel hoof kicked him. Blood printed his brow.

Jim hissed, rolled, thrashed, Will riding him hard, pressing him to grass, trading yell for yell, both fright-pale, heart ramming heart. Electric bolts from the switch flushed up in white stars a gush of fireworks. The carousel spun thirty, spun forty – 'Will, let me up!' – spun fifty times. The calliope howled, boiled steam, ran ancient dry, then played nothing, its keys gibbering as only chitterings boiled up through the vents. Lightning unravelled itself over the sweated outflung boys, delivered flame to the silent horse stampede to light their way around, around with the figure lying on the platform no longer a boy but a man no longer a man but more than a man and even more and even more, much more than that, around, around.

'He's, he's, oh he's, oh look, Will, he's –' gasped Jim, and began to sob, because it was the only thing to do, locked down, nailed tight. 'Oh God, Will, get up! We *got* to make it run backwards!'

Ray Bradbury *Something Wicked This Way Comes*

Childhood's End

(Jan is the last human being left alive. He has survived a little longer than the rest of the human race because he has spent some years on a journey to a distant star. He returns to Earth in a space ship controlled by a race of super-beings, called Overlords. Rashaverak and Karellen are the chief Overlords.)

It was Rashaverak who brought him the news, but he had already guessed it. In the small hours of the morning a nightmare had awakened him, and he had not been able to regain sleep. He could not remember the dream, which was very strange, for he believed that all dreams could be recalled if one tried hard enough immediately after waking. All that he could remember of this was that he had been a small boy again, on a vast and empty plain, listening to a great voice calling in an unknown language.

The dream had disturbed him: he wondered if it was the first onslaught of loneliness upon his mind. Restlessly he walked out of the villa on to the neglected lawn.

A full moon bathed the scene with a golden light so brilliant that he could see perfectly. The immense gleaming cylinder of Karellen's ship lay beyond the buildings of the Overlord base, towering above them and reducing them to man-made proportions. Jan looked at the ship, trying to recall the emotions it had once roused in him. There was a time when it had been an unattainable goal, a symbol of all that he had never really expected to achieve. And now it meant nothing.

How quiet and still it was! The Overlords, of course, would be as active as ever, but for the moment there was no sign of them. He might have been alone on Earth – as indeed in a very real sense he was. He glanced up at the Moon, seeking some familiar sight on which his thoughts could rest.

There were the ancient, well-remembered seas. He had been forty light-years into space, yet had never walked on those silent, dusty plains less than two light-seconds away. For a moment he amused himself trying to locate the crater Tycho. When he did discover it, he was puzzled to find that gleaming speck further from the centre line of the disc than he had thought. And it was then that he realized that the dark oval of the Mare Crissium was missing altogether.

The face that her satellite now turned towards the Earth was not the one that had looked down on the world since the dawn of life. The Moon had begun to turn upon its axis.

That could mean only one thing. On the other side of the Earth, in the land they had stripped so suddenly of life, *they* were emerging from their long trance. As a waking child may stretch its arms to greet the day, they too were flexing their muscles and playing with their new-found powers . . . .

'You have guessed correctly,' said Rashaverak. 'It is no longer safe for us to stay. They may ignore us still, but we cannot take the risk. We leave as soon as our equipment can be loaded – probably in two or three hours.'

He looked up at the sky, as if afraid that some new miracle was about to blaze forth. But all was peaceful: the Moon had set, and only a few clouds rode high upon the west wind.

'It does not matter greatly if they tamper with the Moon,' Rashaverak added, 'but suppose they begin to interfere with the Sun? We shall leave our instruments behind, of course, so that we can learn what happens.'

'I shall stay,' said Jan abruptly. 'I have seen enough of the universe. There's only one thing I'm curious about now – and that is the fate of my own planet.'

Very gently, the ground trembled underfoot.

'I was expecting that,' Jan continued. 'If they alter the Moon's spin, the angular momentum must go somewhere. So the Earth is slowing down. I don't know which puzzles me more – *how* they are doing it, or why.'

'They are still playing,' said Rashaverak. 'What logic is there in the actions of a child? And in many ways the entity that your race has become is still a child. It is not yet ready to unite with the Overmind. But very soon it will be, and then you will have the Earth to your own.

He did not complete the sentence, and Jan finished it for him.

'If, of course, the Earth still exists.'

'You realize that danger – and yet you will stay?'

'Yes. I have been home five – or is it six? – years now. Whatever happens, I'll have no complaints.'

'We were hoping,' began Rashaverak slowly, 'that you would wish to stay. There is something that you can do for us. . . .'

The glare of the Stardrive dwindled and died, somewhere out there beyond the orbit of Mars. Along that road, thought Jan, he alone had travelled, out of all the billions of human beings who had lived and died on Earth. And no one would ever travel it again.

The world was his. Everything he needed – all the material possessions anyone could ever desire – were his for the taking. But he was no longer interested. He feared neither the loneliness of the deserted planet, nor the presence that still rested here in the last moments before it went to seek its unknown heritage. In the inconceivable backwash of that departure, Jan did not expect that he and his problems would long survive.

That was well. He had done all that he had wished to do, and to drag out a pointless life on this empty world would have been unbearable anticlimax. He could have left with the Overlords, but for what purpose? For he knew, as no one else had ever known, that Karellen spoke the truth when he had said: 'The stars are not for Man.'

He turned his back on the night and walked through the vast entrance of the Overlord base. Its size affected him not in the least: sheer immensity no longer had any power over his mind. The lights were burning redly, driven by energies that could feed them for ages yet. On either side lay machines whose secrets he would never know, abandoned by the Overlords in their retreat. He went past them, and clambered awkwardly up the great steps until he had reached the control room.

The spirit of the Overlords still lingered here: their machines were still alive, doing the bidding of their now far-distant masters. What could he add, wondered Jan, to the information they were already hurling into space?

He climbed into the great chair and made himself as comfortable as he could. The microphone, already alive, was waiting for him: something that was the equivalent of a TV camera must be watching, but he could not locate it.

Beyond the desk and its meaningless instrument panels, the wide windows looked out into the starry night, across a valley sleeping beneath a gibbous moon, and to the distant range of mountains. A river wound along the valley, glittering here and there as the moonlight struck upon some patch of troubled water. It was all so peaceful. It might have been thus at Man's birth as it now was at his ending.

Out there across unknown millions of kilometres of space, Karellen would be waiting. It was strange to think that the ship of the Overlords was racing away from Earth almost as swiftly as his signal could speed after it. Almost – but not quite. It would be a long chase, but his words would catch the Supervisor and he would have repaid the debt he owed.

How much of this, Jan wondered, had Karellen planned, and how much was masterful improvisation? Had the Supervisor deliberately let him escape into space, almost a century ago, so that he could return to play the role he was fulfilling now? No, that seemed too fantastic. But Jan was certain now, that Karellen was involved in some vast and complicated plot. Even while he served it, he was studying the Overmind with all the instruments at his command. Jan suspected that it was not only scientific curiosity that inspired the Supervisor: perhaps the Overlords had dreams of one day escaping from their peculiar bondage, when they had learned enough about the powers they served.

That Jan could add to that Knowledge by what he was now doing seemed hard to believe. 'Tell us what you see,' Rashaverak had said. 'The picture that reaches your eye will be duplicated by our cameras. But the message that enters your brain may be very different, and it could tell us a great deal.' Well, he would do his best.

'Still nothing to report,' he began. 'A few minutes ago I saw the trail of your ship disappear in the sky. The Moon is just past full, and almost half its familiar side has now turned from Earth – but I suppose you already know that.'

Jan paused, feeling slightly foolish. There was something incongruous, even faintly absurd, about what he was doing. Here was the climax of all history, yet he might have been a radio commentator at a race track or a boxing ring. Then he shrugged his shoulders and put the thought aside. At all moments of greatness, he suspected, bathos had never been very far away – and certainly he alone could sense its presence here.

'There have been three slight quakes in the last hour,' he continued. 'Their control of the Earth's spin must be marvellous, but not quite perfect. . . . You know, Karellen, I'm going to find it very hard to say anything your instruments haven't already told you. It might have helped if you'd given me some idea of what to expect, and warned me how long I may have to wait. If nothing happens, I'll report again in six hours, as we arranged –

'Hello! They must have been waiting for you to leave. Something's started to happen. The stars are becoming dimmer. It's as if a great cloud is coming up, very swiftly, over all the sky. But it isn't really a cloud. It seems to have some sort of structure – I can glimpse a hazy network of lines and bands that keep changing their positions. It's almost as if the stars are tangled in a ghostly spider's web.'

'The whole network is beginning to glow – to pulse with light, exactly as if it were alive. And I suppose it is: or is it something as much beyond life as *that* is above the inorganic world?

'The glow seems to be shifting to one part of the sky – wait a minute while I move round to the other window.

'Yes – I might have guessed. There's a great burning column, like a tree of fire, reaching above the western horizon. It's a long way off, right round the world. I know where it springs from: *they're* on their way at last, to become part of the Overmind. Their probation is ended: they're leaving the last remnants of matter behind.

'As that fire spreads upwards from the Earth, I can see the network becoming firmer and less misty. In places, it seems almost solid – yet the stars are still shining faintly through it.

'I've just realized. It's not exactly the same, but the thing I saw shooting up above your world, Karellen, was very much like this. Was that part of the Overmind? I supposed you hid the truth from me so that I would have no preconceived ideas – so that I'd be an unbiased observer. I wish I knew what your cameras were showing you now, to compare it with what my mind imagines I'm seeing!

'Is this how it talks to you, Karellen, in colours and shapes like these? I've remembered the control screens on your ships and the patterns that went across them, speaking to you in some visual language which your eyes could read.

'Now it looks exactly like the curtains of the aurora, dancing and flickering across the stars. Why, that's what it really is, I'm sure – a great auroral storm. The whole landscape is lit up – it's brighter than day – reds and golds and greens are chasing each other across the sky – oh it's beyond words, it doesn't seem fair that I am the only one to see it – I never thought such colours –

'The storm's dying down, but the great misty network is still there. I think that aurora was only a by-product of whatever energies are being released up there on the frontier of space. . . .

'Just a minute : I've noticed something else. *My weight's decreasing.* What does that mean ? I've dropped a pencil. It's falling slowly. Something's happened to gravity – there's a great wind coming up – I can see the trees tossing their branches down there in the valley.

'Of course – the atmosphere's escaping. Sticks and stones are rising into the sky, almost as if the Earth itself is trying to follow *them* out into space. There's a great cloud of dust, whipped up by the gale. It's becoming hard to see . . . perhaps it will clear in a a moment.

'Yes – that's better. Everything movable has been stripped away – the dust clouds have vanished. I wonder how long this building will stand ? And it's getting hard to breathe – I must try and talk more slowly.

'I can see clearly again. That great burning column is still there, but it's constricting, narrowing – it looks like the funnel of a tornado, about to retract into the clouds. And – oh this is hard to describe, but just then I felt a great wave of emotion sweep over me. It wasn't joy or sorrow ; it was a sense of fulfilment, achievement. Did I imagine it ? Or did it come from outside ? I don't know.

'And now – *this* can't be all imagination – the world feels empty. Utterly empty. It's like listening to a radio set that's suddenly gone dead. And the sky is clear again – the misty web has gone. What world will it go to next, Karellen ? And will you be there to serve it still ?

'Strange : everything around me is unaltered. I don't know why, but somehow I thought that –'

Jan stopped. For a moment he struggled for words, then closed his eyes in an effort to regain control. There was no room for fear or panic now : he had a duty to perform – a duty to Man, and a duty to Karellen.

Slowly at first, like a man waking from a dream, he began to speak.

'The buildings round me – the ground – the mountains – everything's like glass – *I can see through it*. Earth's dissolving – my weight has almost gone. You were right – they've finished playing with their toys.

'It's only a few seconds away. There go the mountains, like wisps of smoke. Goodbye, Karellen, Rashaverak – I am sorry for you. Though I cannot understand it, I've seen what my race became. Everything we ever achieved has gone up there into the stars. Perhaps that's what the old religions were trying to say. But they got it all wrong: they thought mankind was so important, yet we're only one race in – do *you* know how many? Yet now we've become something that you could never be.

'There goes the river. No change in the sky, though. I can hardly breathe. Strange to see the Moon still shining up there. I'm glad they left it, but it will be lonely now –.

'The light! From *beneath* me – inside the Earth – shining upward, through the rocks, the ground, everything – growing brighter, brighter, blinding –.'

In a soundless concussion of light, Earth's core gave up its hoarded energies. For a little while the gravitational waves crossed and recrossed the Solar System, disturbing ever so slightly the orbits of the planets. Then the Sun's remaining children pursued their ancient paths once more, as corks floating on a placid lake ride out the tiny ripples set in motion by a falling stone.

There was nothing left of Earth. *They* had leeched away the last atoms of its substance. It had nourished them, through the fierce moments of their inconceivable metamorphosis, as the food stored in a grain of wheat feeds the infant plant while it climbs towards the Sun.

Six thousand million miles beyond the orbit of Pluto, Karellen sat before a suddenly darkened screen. The record was complete, the mission ended; he was homeward bound for the world he had left so long ago. The weight of centuries was upon him, and a sadness that no logic could dispel. He did not mourn for Man; his sorrow was for his own race, forever barred from greatness by forces it could not overcome.

For all their achievements, thought Karellen, for all their mastery of the physical universe, his people were no better than a tribe that had passed its whole existence upon some flat and dusty plain. Far off were the mountains, where power and beauty dwelt, where the thunder sported above the glaciers and the air was clear and keen. There the sun still walked, transfiguring the peaks with glory, when all the land below was wrapped in darkness. And they could only watch and wonder: they could never scale those heights.

Yet, Karellen knew, they would hold fast until the end: they would await without despair whatever destiny was theirs. They would serve the Overmind because they had no choice, but even in that service they would not lose their souls.

The great control screen flared for a moment with sombre, ruby light: without conscious effort, Karellen read the message of its changing patterns. The ship was leaving the frontiers of the Solar System: the energies that powered the Stardrive were ebbing fast, but they had done their work.

Karellen raised his hand, and the picture changed once more. A single brilliant star glowed in the centre of the screen: no one could have told, from this distance, that the Sun had ever possessed planets or that one of them had now been lost. For a long time Karellen stared back across that swiftly widening gulf, while many memories raced through his vast and labyrinthine mind. In silent farewell, he saluted the men he had known, whether they had hindered or helped him in his purpose.

No one dared disturb him or interrupt his thoughts: and presently he turned his back upon the dwindling Sun.

Arthur C. Clarke *Childhood's End*

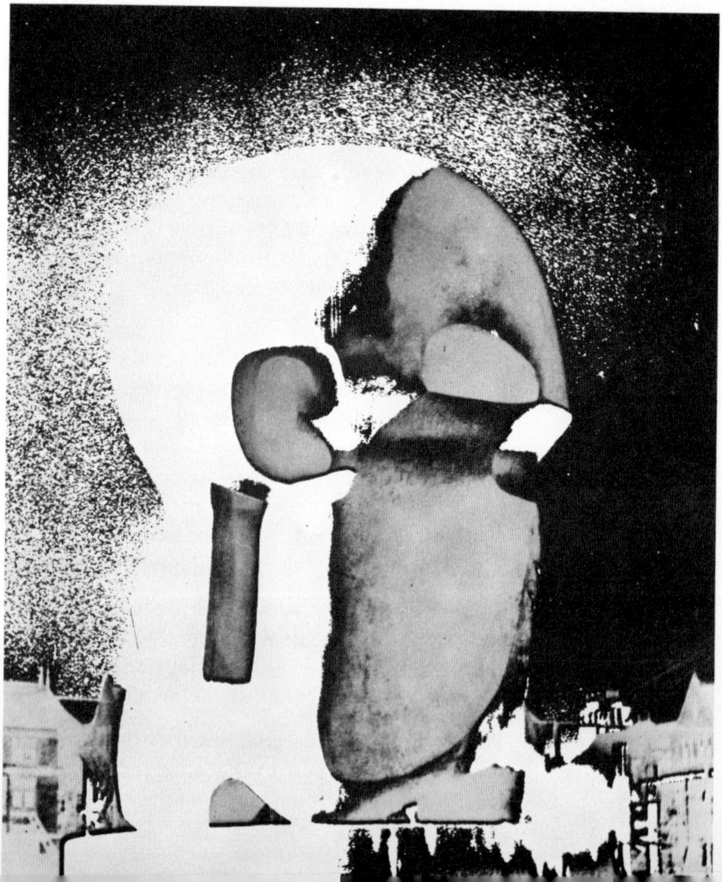

Old Crock

I am the very last astronaut, listen:
I send back messages from obscure planets;
smoke rises from the burning leaves,
something goes liquid beyond my reach.

I am the very last astronaut, listen:
I came here, surfacing like a whale
through oceans alchemists made real.

Listen: space bugs scrape around the cockpit,
terror leaks in, spilling about the controls;
lice block the air tubes, eat into my brain.

I have forgotten my space pills, I
might explode.

About the brain: most is machinery anyway.
No worry there; only the memory now
feels soft and edible.

My only fear: that lice might nest there,
eat out the shapes I've carried with me.
Still now I sense my loneliness breaking.

Now someone else has arrived here,
space-jaunted naked, sits invisible here.
I'm obsolete he tells me, holds up a mirror.

I am the very last astronaut, listen:
skull-white I grin,
skull-white and obviously mad.

Outside there are children playing
like this blackness were a park,
dancing, their songs numerical –

I am too many centuries old.

In the brain-pan bits of machinery float,
still active, trying to get out the holes
where my eyes have been.

Brian Patten

The Mapmaker on his Art

After the bronzed, heroic traveller
Returns to the television interview
And cocktails at the Ritz, I, in my turn,
Set forth across the clean, uncharted paper.
Smiling a little at his encounters with
Savages, bugs, and snakes, for the most part
Skipping his night thoughts, philosophic notes,
Rainy reflections, I translate his trip
Into my native tongue of bearing, shapes,
Directions, distances. My fluent pen
Wanders and cranks as his great river does,
Over the page, making the lonely voyage
Common and human. This, my modest art,
Brings wilderness well down into the range
Of any budget. Under the haunted mountain
Where he lay in delirium, deserted
By his safari, they will build hotels
In a year or two. I make no claim that this
Much matters (they will name a hotel for him,
Not me), yet, lest in the comparison
I should appear a trifle colourless,
I write the running river a rich blue
And – let imagination rage! – wild green
The jungles with their tawny meadows and swam
Where, till the day I die, I will not go.

Howard Nemerov

Acknowledgements

Poems and Prose

For permission to use copyright material acknowledgement is made to the following:

For 'Hard Travelling' by Louis Banks from *Hard Times* by Studs Terkel © 1970 Studs Terkel to Penguin Books Ltd; for 'Seeing the Doctor' from *A Fortunate Man* by John Berger © 1967, 1969 John Berger and Jean Mohr to Penguin Books Ltd; for 'Becoming a Human Being' from *Little Big Man* by Thomas Berger to Eyre & Spottiswoode; for the extract from *When the War Was Over* by Heinrich Boll to Weidenfeld & Nicolson; for 'The Time Merry-Go-Round' from *Something Wicked This Way Comes* by Ray Bradbury to Rupert Hart-Davis Ltd; for 'Ogun' from *Rights of Passage* by Edward Brathwaite to Oxford University Press; for 'The Emigrants' from *Islands* by Edward Brathwaite to Oxford University Press; for 'Limitations' from *Akenfield* by Ronald Blythe to Penguin Books Ltd; for 'A Union Man' by Jack Chaplesworth, first published in *New Society*, to the author; for the extract from *Childhood's End* by Arthur C. Clarke to Sidgwick & Jackson Ltd; for 'Coco' by Larry Coles from *Street Kids* to International Famous Agency; for 'The Boy in the Slums' by Alvin Lewis Curry quoted in *36 Children* to Victor Gollancz; for 'Illuminations' from *Order to View* by René Cutforth © 1969 René Cutforth to Deborah Rogers Ltd; for 'He and I' from *Le Piccole Virtu* by Natalia Ginzburg to Giulio Einaudi Editore; for 'Miss Pringle' from *Free Fall* by William Golding to Faber & Faber Ltd; for 'A Horror Story' by Rod Harrod to the author; for 'Lizards and Snakes' from *Hard House* by Anthony Hecht to Oxford University Press; for 'Suffering' and 'A History Lesson' from *Selected Poems* by Mivoslav Holub translated by Ian Milner and George Theiner to Penguin Books Ltd; for 'A Modest Proposal' from *The Hawk in the Rain* by Ted Hughes to Faber & Faber Ltd; for 'Two Friends' from *Hard Earth* by David Ignatow to Rapp & Whiting; for 'Teaching' from *36 Children* by Herbert Kohl to Victor Gollancz; 'Plague Burial' from *The Painted Bird* by Jerry Kosinski to W. H. Allen & Co. Ltd; for 'Before one goes through the gate' from *Knots* by R. D. Laing to Tavistock Publications Ltd; for 'The Threepenny Tip' by Mark Maplethorpe from the *Daily Mirror* Children's Literary Competition to the *Daily Mirror;* for 'Sent Away to Service' from *Fenland Chronicle* by Sybil Marshall to Cambridge University Press; for 'The Mapmaker on his Art' by Howard Nemerov to Laurence Polinger Ltd; for 'Old Crock' from *Notes to the Hurrying Man* by Brian Patten to George Allen & Unwin Ltd; for 'You're' from *Ariel* by Sylvia Plath to Faber & Faber Ltd; for 'The Adams Family' from *The Watcher on the Cast-Iron Balcony* by Hal Porter to Faber & Faber Ltd; for 'My Thoughts' by Sarah Gristwood from the *Daily Mirror* Children's Literary Competition to the *Daily Mirror*; for 'An Evening at the Garibaldi' from *The Unpriviledged* by Jeremy Seabook to Longman Group Ltd; for the extract from *The Housing Lark* by Samuel Selvon to MacGibbon & Kee; for 'Uvlunaq's Song' from *The Netsilk* edited by Knud Rasmussen to the editor; for 'Slightly Unstuck in Time' from *Slaughterhouse-Five* by Kurt Vonnegut to Jonathan Cape Ltd.

Pictures For the picture on page 3 to John Diele; pages 8–9 to Freddy Fox, courtesy Shell Research Ltd; pages 10–11, 36, 40–41, 44–5 to Magnum Photos; pages 12–13 to Jerry Uelsmann; pages 14–15 Mansell Collection; pages 16–17, 21 to Radio Times Hulton Picture Library, pages 22–3 to the Museum of Modern Art, New York; page 25 to the British Museum, London; pages 26–7 to the West-Baffin Eskimo Cooperative, Cape Dorset; pages 28–9 to the Royal Museum for Fine Art, Antwerp; page 32 to Paul Popper Ltd; pages 35, 93 to Keystone Press Agency Ltd; pages 52–3, 55, 56–7 to Jean Mohr; pages 66–7 to Frank Lane; pages 68–9, 72–3 to the Notman Photographic Archives; page 75 to World Health Organization; page 91 to Robert George Jackson III from *36 Children* by Herbert Kohl published by Victor Gollancz Ltd; pages 98–9 to Mr Eglon-Shaw, the Sutcliffe Gallery, Whitby, Yorkshire; pages 94–5 to Bill Brandt; pages 100–101, 104 to the Bettmann Archieves Inc.; pages 103–4 to Culver Pictures Inc.; pages 108–9 to Patrick Ward; page 113 to the Tate Gallery, London; page 120 to Chicago University.

Every effort has been made to trace owners of copyright material, but in some cases this has not proved possible. The publishers would be glad to hear from any further copyright owners of material reproduced in *Openings*.

List of Illustrations

Index

Authors, Translators and Collectors